LEE YING HO 李英豪

ANTIQUE
CERAMICS

古董瓷器

Translated by Goh Beng Choo

ASIAPAC • SINGAPORE

Publisher
ASIAPAC BOOKS PTE LTD
629 Aljunied Road
#04-06 Cititech Industrial Building
Singapore 389838
Tel: (65) 7453868
Fax: (65) 7453822

Original Chinese edition
First published 1992 as 古董瓷器
Copyright © 1992 by Lee Ying Ho

English translation right: Published by agreement with
Publications (Holdings) Limited, Hong Kong
All rights reserved.

This English edition
© 1996 ASIAPAC BOOKS, SINGAPORE
ISBN 981-3029-86-2

First published January 1996

Cover design by Bay Song Lin & Jonathan Yip
Body text in 8.9pt Palatino
Printed in Singapore by Loi Printing Pte Ltd

Publisher's Note

Singapore is becoming more affluent and is now a fast-growing arts centre for the region.

Already, we have seen evidences of the expansion of the local art industry: art exhibitions, art auctions, arts performances, and the setting up of the National Arts Council.

In keeping with the aspiration for finer things, we are pleased to launch the new Asiapac Collectors' Series, beginning with *Antique Ceramics* and *Jadeite*, both written by established Hong Kong art critic Lee Ying Ho. We hope that this series will help to enhance the reader's enjoyment of Chinese art and collector's items.

We would like to express our gratitude to Ms Goh Beng Choo for the translation, and the production team for putting in their best efforts in this publication.

Acknowledgement

We are indebted to Christie, Manson & Woods Ltd. and Sotheby's Holdings Inc. for granting Mr Lee Ying Ho the permission to reproduce their materials on ceramic wares contained in this translated version, without which this edition will not be possible.

About the Author

Lee Ying Ho, a native of Guangdong Zhongshan, was born in 1941. From an early age, he has loved art and travelling. He was, at various times, chairman of the Hong Kong Modern Literature and Fine Art Association, chairman of the International Painting Salon; Asian consultant to The World Collectors' Association, The International Orchid-Growing Association, and The World Horticulture Centre. He is one of the famous "Four Eccentrics of Hong Kong", and became well known for his art critiques after the late 1960s.

He went into semi-retirement in the early 1970s, studying ancient Chinese books, cats, dogs, fish and flowers. He started writing again in the mid 1980s, and upon his marriage to Xia Shumin, resumed his carefree life. Husband and wife travelled widely and collected antique watches, antique ceramics, jade, stamps, Yixing tea pots, sea-shells, Tianhuang seal stones and embroidery.

Mr Lee's writings on collectibles, animals and flowers have been featured in major newspapers. Some of his articles include *The Visual Side of Critique, A Mountain Over Another* and *Orchid Growing*. He has also hosted several programmes on television and radio, including *The Joy of Collecting* and *The Art of Living*.

About the Translator

Goh Beng Choo, a Singaporean, received her BA degree in Arts & Social Sciences from the University of Singapore (now known as the National University of Singapore).

Ms Goh once worked as a bilingual journalist with *The Straits Times*, Singapore's leading newspaper. She was attached to the *Bilingual Desk*, Section Two of the paper, where she reported and reviewed arts and literary events organized in Singapore, Hong Kong and Taiwan, in English and Chinese languages.

Now a freelance journalist and translator (Chinese/English) with special interest in fine arts, she has translated into English *The Sayings of Zhuang Zi* by Tsai Chih Chung, and an award-winning novel entitled *A Man Like Me* by Singapore author Yeng Pway Ngon.

Her latest translation works include *Antique Ceramics* and *Jadeite* by Lee Ying Ho.

Contents

THE BASIS FOR AUTHENTICATION

Part I

An early Ming blue-and-white moonflask.
Yongle. 26.7cm. high.
Valued at approximately HK$7 million.
Featured in a Christie's Swire auction.

明初永樂**青花花卉紋扁壺**，
高26.7厘米，曾在太古佳士得拍賣，
價值約七百萬港元。

right: A fencai gourd-shaped
vase with butterflies. Qianlong.
23cm. high.

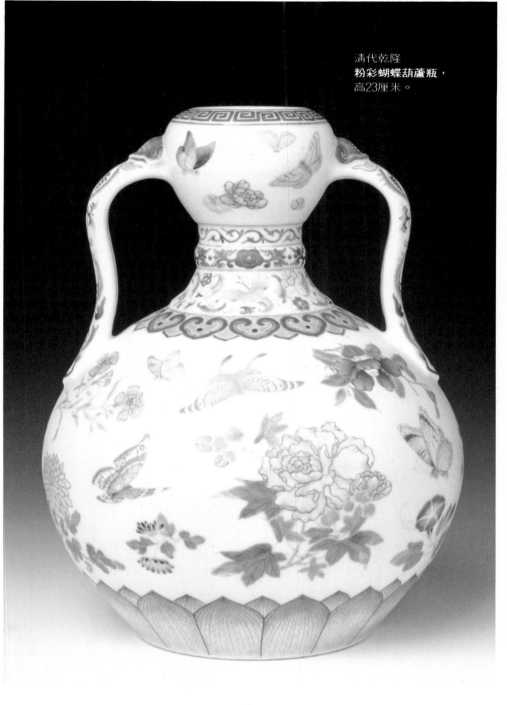

清代乾隆
粉彩蝴蝶葫蘆瓶，
高23厘米。

清代乾隆**粉彩葫蘆瓶**，
高36.9厘米，曾在太古
佳士得拍賣，價值約三百萬港元。

A fencai double-gourd vase. Qianlong. 36.9cm. high. Valued at HK$3 million. Featured in a Christie's Swire auction.

清乾隆**黃地青花**梅瓶。

A yellow-ground blue-and-white mei ping. Qianlong.

5

貴重罕見的**粉彩花瓶**，
清乾隆年製，高40厘米(15¾吋)

6

Fine Official Wares are the Ultimate Choice

When it comes to ceramics collecting, it is important to be very discriminating. If possible, do not buy popular wares. Of course there are occasionally good pieces among popular wares, but the problem is that in the antique ceramics market, popular wares have limited appeal and even the rarer pieces do not fetch good prices.

A knowledgeable collector demands perfection, genuine antiquity and originality in ceramics. Official wares are safe bets because their production was supervised by experts under stringent conditions.

There is a limited quantity of official wares and the fine ones are endowed with a fine, smooth, even and solid clay body without flaws. The material used in making official wares is fine and exquisite. The colour of the glaze is rich, pure, brilliant and evenly toned. Body and glaze are perfectly fused. When we hold the ware, we can feel a smoothness without stickiness, and the weight should feel right. Official wares are noted for their beautiful motifs which are vivid, lively and tactile. The brushstrokes are detailed and fluid with a sense of rhythm, much like that of a good Chinese painting. The craftsmanship is superb and the ware well-shaped.

Do not buy official wares that are flawed, broken at the rim, uneven at the base or cracked. The finest official wares are those produced during the Yuan dynasty (excluding those decorated in extremely sombre-coloured glaze) and the Hongwu, Yongle, Xuande and Chenghua periods of the Ming dynasty. Official wares produced after the Hongzhi period are generally of poor quality. Among Qing dynasty wares, attention should focus on those of the Kangxi, Yongzheng and Qianlong periods. The craft declined after the Jiaqing period. Official wares made after the Yongle period have a reign mark, which should be examined carefully when you make your selection.

left: A rare and expensive fencai vase. Qianlong mark and of the period. 40cm. high.

A blue-and-white bowl with phoenix. Xuande. 20cm. diam.

明代宣德
青花鳳凰紋盤，
口徑20厘米。

An enamelled bowl with flowers. Qing dynasty, Yongzheng mark and of the period.

清代雍正
琺瑯彩花卉紋盌，
宮廷御製。

bottom: A rare fencai yellow-ground bowl with floral design. Qing dynasty, Qianlong mark and of the period.

清乾隆官窰**黃地**
粉彩花卉紋盌，罕有。

Using Your Sense of Touch

In selecting antique ceramics, the use of hands, eyes and ears helps in authentication.

Good quality ware should feel smooth and fine. The weight is also a useful indicator of the date of the ware. Wares of the Ming Xuande reign are heavier than those of the Yongle period while those from Yuan dynasty are generally heavier than those of the Yongle, Xuande and Chenghua periods.

Among Qing dynasty wares, the body of Kangxi *wucai* (famille verte) ware is fine, compact and proportionate to its weight. Yongzheng ware, including those in *fencai* (famille rose), blue-and-white, and *doucai* (contrasting colours), are generally lighter and thinner. The bigger ones may be well potted but are never thick or heavy. Recent fakes are heavier. Qianlong ware may vary in thickness but the good ones are delicate and evenly potted. Imitations of Qianlong ware have thin vessel walls and coarse bodies. Wares of the early Jiaqing reign retained the fineness of Qianlong ware but those produced in late Jiaqing are clumsy and coarse. Wares of the Daoguang period are lighter but their bodies are thick and awkward.

A blue-and-white gourd-shaped moonflask. Yongle. 29.5cm. high.

明代永樂
青花葫蘆式雙耳扁瓶
高29.5厘米。
（用「手感」
可知瓷器
胎質是否
幼滑均勻）

A blue-and-white spittoon with waves. Xuande. 15.2cm. high.

明代宣德
青花海濤紋渣斗，
高15.2厘米。
（鑑別瓷器要靠「手感」。）

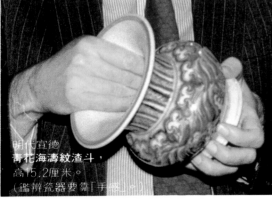

9

A Qianlong fencai celadon-ground moulded
lobed vase with floral design in panels. 36.2cm.
high. Valued at HK$4 million. Featured in a
Christie's Swire auction.

清代乾隆**粉青地開光花卉尊**，
高36.2厘米，曾在太古
佳士得拍賣，
價值約四百萬港元。

Listening for the Ringing Sound

The sound which a porcelain piece makes when struck is important. Some experts can tell if a piece has cracks just by tapping it lightly. Genuine Song dynasty black glaze round vessels produced in Jizhou kilns make a deep, hoarse sound when tapped whereas fakes sound "cold" and ironically clear due to differences in the quality of clay.

Fakes of the coloured and blue-and-white Qianlong wares have thin walls and porous glazes. Hence, they are unable to produce the deep and solid sound made by the authentic pieces. Because of even potting and consistent thickness, official wares sound the same wherever you tap. Fakes, on the contrary, produce different sounds when tapped at different places.

In general, wares without cracks should produce a loud ringing sound when tapped but there are exceptions such as Jizhou black glaze wares which may make a dull, light thudding sound. Besides listening, the authenticator should also take note of the form, glaze, mark, motif and quality of clay and glaze before he assesses the ware.

明代**青花罐**，
有明顯的沖口。

A Ming blue-and-white
jar with visible rim
chips.

清代乾隆**釉裏紅葫蘆形花瓶**。

An underglazed red gourd-shaped vase. Qianlong.

清代乾隆
琺瑯彩開光長頸鼓腹花瓶,
主題以雲蝠爲背景,
非常罕有,高19.2厘米。

12

Using the Magnifying Glass

Because some fakes were skilfully produced, the use of a 10X magnifying glass under a bright light to examine the ware would help in authentication. Examine the glaze in particular - porous and dry glaze often gives the fakes away. Rough or uneven glaze with varying thickness may mean the piece is an imitation or a product of a poor quality private kiln.

Use the magnifying glass to examine the exposed clay at the foot or mouth of the piece. Ming dynasty wares, with very few exceptions, almost always show yellow crack lines (firing haircracks). Most of the Ming blue-and-white wares have a brilliant green glaze which is a greenish colour over white, and a clear and smooth look. The magnifying glass can also help in distinguishing minute differences in the brushstrokes of the reign mark.

The bubbles on the reign mark can give useful clues too. Reign marks on Ming dynasty Chenghua wares contain pearl-shape bubbles while fakes of Qing dynasty wares have varying bubbles and a hazy green reign mark. This obvious flaw is even more prominent in fakes from the early Republic of China. The magnifying glass should be used to examine the interior of the ware as well since a fake may have a flawless exterior.

left: A very rare enamelled long-necked globular vase with floral design in panels. Qianlong. 19.2cm. high.

A pair of bowls in opaque enamels with hundred flowers. Yongzheng. 10.8cm. diam.

清代雍正
琺瑯彩「百花圖」盌一對，
直徑10.8厘米。

明代永樂**青花瓜紋碟**，
曾在蘇富比拍賣。

**A Ming Yongle blue-and-white
dish with melons. Featured in a
Sotheby's auction.**

Glossy Surfaces of Fake Wares

If you hold a piece of porcelain ware to the light and see a colourful halo on the surface of the glaze or a faint red lustre commonly known as "clam light", you can be sure it is an official ware of early Qing.

Recent fakes do not have that halo and their surface exudes a dazzling gloss known as "fiery light". Like the ageing of wine, an antique porcelain ware that is more than two hundred years old displays glaze that is mellow with a subtle lustre and which fuses perfectly with the clay. Nevertheless, lack of evidence of that dazzling gloss alone does not guarantee the authenticity of the ware because some imitations of early Qing ware have lost that surface gloss.

Fake "archaic wares" with an unusually pale white colour have been immersed in acid to remove the gloss while others have been soaked for a long time in a solution of tea and soda, which unfortunately, damaged the glaze and dampened its hue. Cow hide and sheep hide have also been used by potters to polish the body of fake wares to remove that surface gloss but this method leaves behind traces of fine parallel crazes which can be detected under the magnifying glass. There should be no fine crazes on the glaze of an original ware.

On the other hand, Ming dynasty ware looks translucent against the light, showing dark red or ivory white colour. Fake wares of late Qing and early Republic of China show a greenish-white colour without the translucence.

清代雍正
仿明初青花大碟

A large dish,
Yongzheng,
imitating early Ming
blue-and-white ware.

明代永樂**青花梅瓶**，
曾在蘇富比拍賣。

CLAY AND GLAZE

Judging the Quality of the Body by the Foot Ring

The components of clay and glaze and methods of firing differed from dynasty to dynasty. Knowing the unique characteristics of wares of each dynasty helps in authentication. Yuan dynasty blue-and-white wares and underglazed red wares, for example, are valued for their pure, white bodies and translucent glazes.

To assess the quality of the body, you need to examine the foot ring which is unglazed; the spot on the body of the piece where the glaze has shrunk is another area to check.

The bodies of wares of the Hongwu period (Ming dynasty) are ponderous with uneven thickness. That of the Yongle wares are smooth and delicate. Wares with ponderous bodies are solid and compact while those with thin bodies are lithe and well-formed. The bodies of Xuande wares are fine and ponderous with sandy bases and few joints. Those of Chenghua ware are pure, brilliant and thin and when held up to the light, show translucent dark red and ivory white colours. Such fine white bodies, when combined with translucent glazes, gives Chenghua wares their classic charm. The bodies of Hongzhi wares are well-formed and fine, having inherited the traits of Chenghua wares.

Unfortunately the quality of clay deteriorated in the Wanli period. The porcelain bodies of Wanli wares are irregularly shaped and are thick, heavy and porous with traces of cracks and oil leakage when examined from the side. On the whole, porcelain bodies of Ming wares are not as compact and pure as that of Qing wares. Qing Kangxi wares reached the zenith of pottery art with pure and jade-like bodies.

left: A blue-and-white mei ping vase. Yongle. Featured in one of Sotheby's auctions.

A rare pale green-glaze Ming bowl on three legs in imitation of Longquan ware. Very rare. Xuande.

明代宣德
冬青釉(仿龍泉青釉)
三足盤，甚罕有。

A yellow-ground blue-and-white vase. Yongzheng. H: 21cm.

18

Dating by the Quality of the Clay

You need to observe the clay carefully when you buy Qing official ware.

Famille verte *(wucai)* wares of Kangxi not only have solid and fine bodies but also a deep, aged lustre which is perfectly natural. Recent fakes are glazed with new pigment and give off a surface gloss without that spontaneous aged glaze tone. This is because Kangxi wares were glazed with pigment left from the Ming dynasty. Makers of fakes in the Guangxu period and early Republic of China could not find the same old glaze material to create that colour tone.

Yongzheng official wares have translucent glazes and clear, white bodies which are well-formed and thin.

You should opt for wares of Kangxi and Yongzheng periods if you want to collect the best of Qing dynasty wares. The bodies of early Qianlong wares are fine and regularly shaped. That of late Qianlong wares are not as translucent, with quality which is somewhat like that of Jiaqing wares.

The late Jiaqing saw the decline of Qing wares and the production of coarse clay; even official wares of this period are clumsy and rough like Daoguang wares. Wares from popular kilns have even poorer quality with uneven shape and thickness. Daoguang wares are porous and rough, and their inferior quality obvious.

Tongzhi wares, too, are coarse and clumsy. They are decorated in rough and impure glazes, and the brushstrokes used for painting the motifs are inferior.

Compared with Daoguang and Tongzhi wares, the bodies of Guangxu official wares are slightly better in quality. But they are nowhere near Kangxi, Yongzheng and Qianlong wares.

清康熙青花
仿米芾畫山水瓶，
高45.7厘米。

A blue-and-white vase with motif painted in imitation of a painting by Mi Fu. Kangxi. H: 45.7cm.

明代永樂**青花盤**，
直徑44厘米。
盤口帶棱口，
較爲少見。
A blue-and-white dish. Yongle.
DM:44cm. Rare rhombus-shaped
rim.

Authentication of Ming Dynasty Ware by the Glaze

To distinguish the quality and tone of glazes, you need to use a 10X magnifying glass, especially if you are checking the size and density of the bubbles. The jade-green Yongle wares show densely-formed bubbles with a very glassy appearance. The glazes are concentrated on the mouth, rim, base of the Yongle white glaze porcelain wares, and where glazes are thin there should be a display of yellow and white colours. Thickly glazed areas should display a subtle green colour due to a higher content of potassium and sodium. These characteristics are not easy to imitate.

The greenish glaze surface of Ming Xuande blue-and-white wares is known as bright green glaze. The bubbles on the glaze surface vary in size and are rather misty like clouds.

The coloured glazes which decorate Xuande wares are fine with a high concentration of bubbles, creating the "orange peel effect". The body and foot of each piece show bright green glaze; while wares produced in later period show less of the orange peel effect. Fakes made in the Qing period show orange peel effect that appears too even and contrived, their glaze bubbles lacking in depth and of the same size. These are elements to watch out for in authenticating porcelain.

Glazes of Chenghua wares are fine like jade, and brilliant, with a subtle green colour on their surface. Fakes of early Republic of China show glazes with impurities and rough surface without the brilliant appearance of glazes of Chenghua wares.

明代宣德**青花歲寒三友盤**。

A blue-and-white dish with three winter friends. Xuande.

明代**青花瓷碟**。

A Ming dynasty blue-and-white dish.

A yellow ground blue-and-white dish with floral design. Yongzheng.

清代雍正
黃地青花花卉紋碟。

Identification of the Glazes of Qing Dynasty Ware

The fine, lustrous, pure and thick glaze of the Yongle period of Ming dynasty and the delicate glaze of the Xuande period with orange-peel texture underwent great changes after the Hongzhi period. Glaze of early Hongzhi is greyish white in colour, that of mid Hongzhi is greenish grey, while late Hongzhi glaze is of a bright green.

By the Wanli period (late Ming) the glaze managed to maintain a thick lustre and a glassy quality in the early stage. It thinned gradually and turned green on the surface.

In the Kangxi period of the Qing dynasty, porcelain glaze resumed its subtle and spontaneous lustre with little impurities. Recent fakes display a flickering light on the surface; the glaze seems murky and hazy, lacking clarity and delicacy. When examined from the side, the *wucai* (famille verte) glaze of Kangxi wares exude a clam light which is technically difficult to imitate.

The tone of the glazes of Yongzheng official wares is invariably pure white. Most of the coloured wares are covered with lustrous glazes in a fine powdery white colour that put them on par with the best glazes of the preceding dynasty.

The glazes of the official wares of Qianlong are firm, clear and even, unlike their porous imitations that display a fiery flicker.

In early Jiaqing period glazes maintained the lustrous surface associated with glazes of late Qianlong but towards the end of the period, glazes looked greenish with no lustre. Some wares display wave-like glazes; others are covered with glazes that are much too thin.

Wave-like glazes became more evident on wares of the Daoguang period, some of which display tiny wrinkles. The glazes are generally porous and not well blended with the clay bodies, and show a powdery white colour. There are few exquisite wares of the Daoguang period. Some wares may be shaped like Kangxi, Yongzheng and Qianlong wares but on closer inspection, reveal numerous flaws. The glazes on them are either too thin or too thick and uneven.

Glaze quality deteriorated further in the Tongzhi period, which made ceramic wares look white, coarse and thick.

Wares of the Guangxu period in imitation of early Qing wares lack lustre and are too thin and porous.

清康熙銅紅花
琺瑯瓷水盅，罕見。

A rare copper red enamelled cup. Kangxi.

明代永樂
青花葫蘆式雙耳扁瓶，
胎與釉均精細，高29.5厘米，
價值約六百萬港元。

FORM

The Elegant Form of Yongle Official Wares

Those who collect Ming Yongle official wares are well aware that the foot ring of this type of ware, which was exposed to the atmosphere in the kiln, usually shows flint-stone red specks, and that both the form of the ware and the foot ring are uniquely styled.

Many of the Yongle blue-and-white wares feature creatures and plants as motifs in lively and powerful manner; their imitations show dull and contrived brushstrokes without fluency and spontaneity.

Yongle official wares are famous for their exquisite, elegant style and come in a larger variety of forms than Yuan and Ming wares, especially chicken bowl (雞心盌) and hand-pressing cup (壓手盃).

The period is noted for the celebrated *tuo tai* wares (脫胎器) that are thin and evenly formed. They are so light and thin that the ancient Chinese likened them to the thin film covering an egg. They also have lower and shorter foot-rims than wares of the succeeding Xuande reign with predominantly small-sized wares.

Most Yongle wares are round-shaped vessels such as saucer, bowl and dish. The edge of the mouths of some of them are sharp instead of round and smooth. Vessels such as jar, flask and container have the right thickness and weight. The imitations produced in the early Republic have coarse clay bodies, their weight being out of proportion to their size.

Because of frequent trade with Persia and Arabia, some Yongle wares show influence of imported wares in form, while others still carried traces of the Yuan Mongolian style. Nevertheless, they have fine, graceful forms quite unlike the thick, heavy wares typical of the Yuan dynasty. The shape of the handleless jug, for example, was derived from the hand washer of Islamic culture. The monk-cap ewer and jar with handles have Arabic inscriptions on them and was possibly for export.

left: A blue-and-white double-earred gourd-shaped flask. Yongle. Very fine body and glaze. H: 29.5cm. Valued at HK$6 million.

A rare blue-and-white bowl with lotus scrolls. Early Yongle.

永樂初期
青花連枝盌，罕有。

明代宣德**青花海濤紋渣斗**，
官窰罕品，高15.2厘米。

A rare Xuande official blue-
and-white spittoon with
pattern of sea waves.

A Xuande yellow-ground
blue-and-white covered jar
with melons and cricket.

明代宣德**黃地**
青花果紋蟋蟀蓋罐，
造型特別，罕有。

The Myriad Forms of Xuande Official Ware

Porcelain wares of each period have their distinctive features which may serve as criteria for authenticating. Small cups of the Ming dynasty, for example, are noted for their daintiness. Their fakes, however, are much larger and sometimes, distorted.

Xuande official wares have an elegant, solid form, large but not clumsy. The stem cups of this period are particularly graceful with a fine sense of balance and steadiness. Bowls, cups and vases make up a large portion of Xuande blue-and-white wares and come in a variety of innovative designs.

The most distinguished types of Ming vases are the globular vase with small neck and big round body, the *dan* vase (膽瓶) with slender neck and round body, the dragon-motif flattened vase, the *mei ping* (梅瓶) with rich motifs and the *yu hu chun* (玉壺春) or pear-shaped, bottle vase. The most outstanding Xuande blue-and-white vase is the flattened gourd vase with ribbon-shaped handles which bears motifs from Central Asian cultures.

The shape of the foot ring of a genuine Xuande ware is rectangular with corners tending to be slightly round; while fakes produced in the Qing dynasty have either oval or rectangular-shaped foot ring. The original ware has horizontal luting on its body, whereas the fakes have vertical luting on the sides.

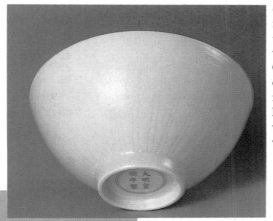

明代宣德
白釉暗紋盌，罕見。

A rare white-glazed bowl with anhua (hidden design). Xuande.

An underglazed red stem cup with pomegranate. Xuande.

明代宣德**釉裏紅**
三多高足盃。

A blue-and-white jar with flowers.
Chenghua. H: 10.5cm. Worth
approx. HK$12 million. Featured
in one of Christie's Swire auctions.

明代成化青花花卉紋罐，
高10.5厘米，曾在太古佳士得拍賣，
懂值約一千二百萬港元。

The Distinctive Forms of Chenghua Ware

A friend of mine who has a blue-and-white covered jar wanted to know if it was an original from the Chenghua period of the Ming dynasty.

On examination I noticed that although the body-and-glaze and motif are of the Chenghua ware style, the cover is an imitation, probably from the late Qing dynasty. Most Chenghua jars were made with lids which have been broken or misplaced in the course of time. Besides, it is well-known that the Chenghua jar lids are slightly domed but not flattened. The jar lids of Qing wares, on the contrary, are flat.

Most Chenghua wares are small ceramic bowls, jars, plates, dishes and cups. Its chicken cup is more famous than its stem cup. Imitations of Chenghua wares feel rough to the touch due to impurities.

Ceramic expert Guo Zizhang says of wares from the Chenghua kilns: "The chicken cup from the Cheng kiln tops the category of wine cups with its motif of poeny on top and that of lively hen-and-chick below. Other types such as wine cups painted with grapes, figures, insects and paper-thin blue-and-white cups are in various tones and solid clay body, all exquisite and attractive."

明成化青花
獅子紋高足盌，
高15厘米，罕有。

The official wares of Chenghua have a lyrical beauty. The jar with the *tian* (天) character decorated with *doucai* is particularly charming; it is marked with *tian* in blue-and-white pigment on the base with no double band.

A blue-and-white stem cup with lions. Chenghua. H: 15cm.

bottom: A yellow-glazed blue-and-white dish with flower-and-fruit. Chenghua.

明代成化
黃釉青花花果盤
（六字橫款）

清代康熙
琺瑯彩黃地花卉紋御製盌，
採用陰影來表達立體感，
罕有，價值約八百萬港元。

A Kangxi official yellow-ground bowl in opaque enamels with flower. Worth approx. HK$8 million.

A pair of bowls in coral red glaze with floral design from the Qing dynasty, Kangxi mark and period.

康熙御製**珊瑚紅地彩盌**一對

The Unique Forms of Kangxi and Yongzheng Wares

The official wares of early Kangxi are often rustic, thick and heavy. By the Yongzheng period, thin porcelain had reached its zenith.

There are some late Kangxi wares which imitate archaic bronze vessels. These could be fish bowls, wine vessels, vases, teapots and bowls.

Many pieces of *wucai* (famille verte) vases, blue-and-white brush pots and porcelain carvings are from the Lang kiln, a kiln associated with Lang Tingji, a renowned supervisor. Subjects such as landscape, flower, insect and legendary figures are vividly depicted. This period boasts some of the finest painted porcelain.

From the Kangxi period onwards, classic essays in the *kai* (regular) style of calligraphy were found on blue-and-white porcelain wares.

The paintings, noted for originality, are influenced by celebrated artists like Chen Laolian, Dong Qichang, Hua Yan and the four Wangs. Most odd-shaped pieces with inferior paintings are imitations or products of popular kilns.

Yongzheng official wares are purer than Kangxi wares. The former are valued for their silvery white body, elegant form and graceful contours. These include the globular vase, pomander, pomegranate-shaped *zun* (尊) vase, peach-shaped washer, and ewer with handle. They are famous for their excellent imitation of Song dynasty glazes.

清康熙**豇豆紅鐣鑼洗**，
直徑12.1厘米，
「大清康熙年製」款。

An underglazed peach-red washer. DM: 12.1cm. Qing dynasty, Kangxi mark and of the period.

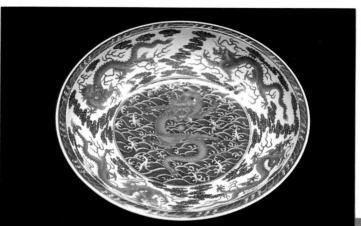

清代乾隆
青花礬紅彩龍紋大瓷盤，
直徑48.2厘米。
（經兩次燒製過程才完成
首先燒青花，再用
低溫燒礬紅彩。）

A blue-and-white large
porcelain dish with vitriol red
enamel and dragons. Qianlong.
DM: 48.2cm.

A blue-and-white
zun lotus scroll.
Qianlong.
H: 45.5cm.

清乾隆**青花**
纏枝番蓮紋尊，
高45.5厘米。

32

From Magnificence to Vulgarity

During the Qianlong period, the Tang kiln further developed its porcelain-making skills which had been handed down from the Kangxi and Yongzheng periods.

Early Qianlong wares have the fine body and form typical of late Yongzheng wares. Late Qianlong pieces suffered a decline in quality but the period does not lack exquisite archaic imitations.

A Record of the Pottery Art of Jingdezhen (chapter 5) commented on the superb pottery art of Qianlong wares: " The clay bodies of the various imitation wares are comparable to the genuine pieces; even their glazes are excellent reproductions of the original. They have superb craftsmanship. A new variety of enamels has also emerged, such as foreign aubergine, pale green, streaked silver, grisaille, foreign enamel, black ground with blue-and-white, black ground with gilt design, sky blue and flambé. The paste of these wares is whitish, free from impurities and the body is generally noted for its balanced thickness and brilliance."

The Qianlong period also produced novel vessels such as revolving vases and wares imitating animals, plants and fruits. Glazes in mocked wood texture, archaic bronze, lacquer and fossilized wood were expertly created.

Unfortunately, towards the close of the period, the designs tended to be elaborate and repetitive. The era after the Jiaqing and Daoguang periods saw a decline in the standard of the wares with only a few fine pieces worth collecting.

A magnificent yellow-ground fencai bowl with floral design. Qianlong.

華麗非凡的乾隆
黃地粉彩花卉紋盌

33

元代**青花印花花果紋棱口大盤**，
完整無缺，極少見，
花紋部分是繪製，
部分是印製，直徑48厘米。

Large Yuan blue-and-white lobed dish
with floral and fruit design. A rare, well-
formed piece, design partly slip-painted
and partly in relief. DM: 48 cm.

DECORATION

The Multi-layered Decoration of Blue-and-White Ware of the Yuan Dynasty

In addition to the famous creamy white *Shufu* (樞府) ware which made the *Jingdezhen* (景德鎮) wares famous, two other types of ware: blue-and-white and a new type of underglazed red, greatly influenced porcelain art of the succeeding dynasties.

Shufu ware is white with a tinge of light green. Its opaque duck's green egg tone earned it the name, "duck's egg green". A genuine *Shufu* porcelain has the characters *"shu fu"* in symmetry amid its slip-painted decorations. *Shufu* wares were no longer produced after the Yuan dynasty.

The green-and-white ware that inherited the fine tradition of Song ware is not as refined, pure and translucent as its predecessor. Its quality declined after the late Ming dynasty.

The most valuable items are the Yuan blue-and-white and a new type of underglazed red ware. However, well-formed, brilliant pieces are rare.

Yuan blue-and-white has excellent multi-layered decoration. The main and secondary motifs are finely balanced.

元代**青花八棱梨形瓶**

A Yuan blue-and-white octagonal pear-shaped vase.

Flowers, landscape and figures were painted in the "Scholar Painter Style", noted for its liveliness, fluidity and variety. Some pieces have carved, slip-painted and embossed designs.

Blue-and-white produced by private kilns have simpler designs and are less valuable. They were made with native cobalt oxide with a higher proportion of cobalt and lower proportion of iron oxide, hence a dark blue colour. The official wares were made with imported cobalt oxide and are brilliant in colour with washes of varying tone.

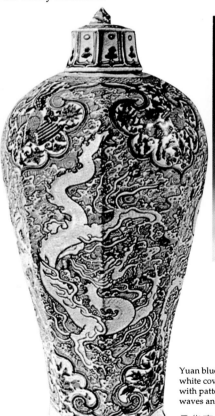

Yuan blue-and-white covered jar with patterns of sea waves and dragon.

元代青花**海水龍紋八棱蓋瓶**

明代洪武青花菊花紋執壺，
完整珍貴，明初青花執壺
比釉裏紅更少見，
價值一千二百萬港元，
曾在蘇富比拍賣。

Decorations of Late Yuan and Early Ming Ware

Experienced collectors know that the fringe decoration on a piece is important in authentication. Each period bears its style and characteristics. The pattern often reveals the custom and lifestyle as it almost always has its distinct calligraphy and painting. A knowledge of Ming and Qing calligraphy as well as painting is helpful in dating porcelain.

Yuan blue-and-white is noted for a vivid, rhythmic, traditional freehand style. Many official wares were obviously influenced by the "Four King Painters" (painter-laureates, namely Huang Gongwang, Wu Zhen, Wang Meng and Ni Zan).

The cloud and dragon motifs on many early Ming Hongwu official wares were inspired by late Yuan jade pieces.

During the Yongle period, the decorations moved towards spontaneity and simplicity. Like the late Yuan pieces, floral designs appeared on the exterior and the interior of Yongle ware, bearing the "dotted flower motif"; only the lotus sprays on Ming wares have larger flowers and smaller leaves. Subjects included bird, flower, fruit, wave, cloud and the dragon-and-phoenix. Cobalt specks visible on the glaze made figure painting unfavourable.

A rare Ming Yongle blue-and-white jar with fruit and flowers.

明代永樂**青花**
折枝花果瓜棱罐，罕有。

left : Ming Hongwu blue-and-white ewer with chrysanthemums. Well-formed and rarer than underglazed red pieces. Valued at HK$12 million. Featured at one of Sotheby's auctions.

明代宣德**青花**棱口龍紋洗子，
直徑18.9厘米。

Ming Xuande blue-and-white
lobed washer with dragon.
DM: 18.9 cm

A rare Ming Yongle blue-and-
white lobed jar with floral
sprays and fruit.

明代永樂**青花**
折枝花果瓜棱罐，罕有。

The Dull, Disjointed and Stiff Brushstrokes on Fakes

According to Geng Baochang, a porcelain authenticator, each period has its distinctive motif and material. Imitations fail to match the originals because of their limited technology and material. Recent Yongle and Xuande fakes lack the smudges and washes of an uneven tone. The glazes lack strength and the brushstrokes are dull, broken, stiff and lifeless.

Fakes are also not decorated with glazes from the Mohammedan blue cobalt. Heap-and-pile spots in the cobalt oozing through the glaze during firing results in uneven metallic smudges visible against the light. Imitations are, however, unsuccessfully dotted and painted to create this effect.

The *anhua* (hidden design) motif of early Ming wares is brilliant and fine but rather hazy. Fakes show artificial white lines.

In the late Qing and early Republic era, imitation Yongle and Xuande wares were stiff, lifeless and lacked fine layering. Emperor Xuande influenced the calligraphy and motif. The dragon design is weakly drawn on fakes.

宣德**青花龍紋僧帽壺**，
高22.3厘米。

Xuande blue-and-white monk's
cap ewer with dragon.
H: 22.3cm.

Ming Xuande blue-and-
white underglazed red
stem cup with sea
creatures.

明代宣德**青花
釉裏紅海獸高足盌**。

明代成化
青花纏枝紋梅瓶，
高26.6厘米。

The Unique Decoration of Chenghua Ware

The distinctive features of Chenghua wares are best described by Sun Yingzhou, an expert authenticator. He identifies the period's *doucai* ware by the following colours: bright and light red, yellow on green and an opaque, thick, brilliant purple. The brilliant purple tone is unique and could not be reproduced on fakes.

The decoration of Chenghua ware is charming and delicate, its floral designs painted in perfect symmetry. Fakes bear coarsely painted designs with uneven double-line on the edge of the mouth and the foot ring.

Official Chenghua blue-and-white is distinguished by the blue-and-white double-line painted on the edge of the mouth and the foot ring. The first double-line on the foot ring is lighter while the one closer to the base is darker. In fakes, both lines have the same tone. Imitation Chenghua wares produced in Yongzheng period had weak and awkward brushwork.

In many Chenghua pieces, the designs are outlined, and a single-toned colour filled in. Only front views of flowers are painted and the leaves are mostly palm-shaped. Figures are monochrome.

明代成化**青花連枝花紋盌**

Ming Chenghua blue-and-white bowl
with lotus sprays.

left : Ming Chenghua blue-and-
white mei ping vase with floral
scroll. H: 26.6cm.

明代正德**波斯紋銘五山筆架**，罕見。

A rare Ming Zhengde brush-rest with design of five mountains and Persian script.

明代萬曆**五彩人物蓋盒**。

Ming Wanli wucai (famille verte) covered jar with painting of figures.

42

The Decoration of Late Ming Official Wares

Quality-wise, late Ming official wares are inferior to Yongle, Xuande and Chenghua wares. However, they are unique in body, glaze, shape and decoration. Due to the popularity of Islam and Taoism, phrases from the Koran or Tibetan scriptures are often used. Designs of *The Eight Immortals* and *The Eight Treasures* are common too. Brush strokes are free and fluid.

Taoist decoration and carving in openwork and relief were popular in Jiajing and Wanli periods. After the Jiajing period, images of big-headed children appeared. The blue-and-white lacked the strict composition in Yongle and Xuande wares and tended to be abbreviated and bright.

Jiajing wares sometimes have only one line round the foot ring. Porcelain bowls often have dragon-and-phoenix motif.

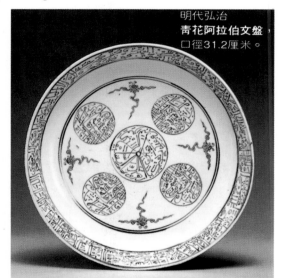

明代弘治
青花阿拉伯文盤，
口徑31.2厘米。

Wanli wares are more elaborate and have animals, plants and figures. However, the dragon motif remains a favourite.

The patterns are finely outlined but the figure and motif are disproportionate, poorly composed and the strokes lifeless and stiff. As collector's items, official Kangxi and Yongzheng wares are better value.

left: Ming Hongzhi blue-and-white dish with Arabic script. DM: 31.2cm.

明萬曆青花梵文直口盌

Ming Wanli blue-and-white bowl in Sanskrit.

明嘉靖青花「福」罐

Ming Jiajing blue-and-white jar with the character "fortune".

清代雍正青花花果紋瓶。

44

Ceramic Decorations of Kangxi, Yongzheng and Qianlong Periods

Porcelain pieces of the Kangxi, Yongzheng and Qianlong periods of the Qing dynasty are famous for richness and variety. The blue-and-white pieces often have bird-and-flower or dragon-and-phoenix designs. Designs were painted freely in a single line but became elaborate during the Qianlong period.

The floral scroll on the blue-and-white Yongzheng and Qianlong wares often have two tones, in an attempt to imitate Ming Xuande blue-and-white. Qianlong porcelain is noted for its jade-like, brilliant colours but are not as finely painted as Kangxi blue-and-white.

Official wares of the three reigns are valued for their translucent and resonant porcelain body, exquisite decoraton and classical beauty. The landscape paintings on Kangxi wares look three dimensional and the mountains are painted in the lively hemp-fibre style. Yongzheng wares are finely painted while Qianlong wares have the magnificence and structure of the Court Painting style.

Qing Yongzheng doucai flared-mouth bowl with decoration of floral scroll. DM: 22.5cm. Six-character Qing Yongzheng mark inside a double circle.

清雍正鬥彩團花
纏枝紋撇口笠式盌，
口徑22.5厘米。
「大清雍正年製」
六字二行雙圈款。

left: Qing Yongzheng blue-and-white vase decorated with fruit and flowers.

明初宣德**花卉紋盌**，罕有。
A rare Xuande blue-and-white bowl with floral design.

bottom: A Xuande blue-and-white lobed washer with dragons (six-character, double-circle mark on base).

明代宣德**青花龍紋葵口洗**
（六字雙行雙圈底款）

IDENTIFICATION BY MARK

The Mark of Yongle and Xuande Periods

Be meticulous when authenticating porcelain. Most of the Jingdezhen wares before the Ming dynasty had no reign marks. This mark only existed from the Yongle period often in the four-character *zhuan* (seal) calligraphic style, and the characters in blue-and-white pigment are tightly and vigorously written.

Nearly all wares with a six-character mark or written in the *kai* (regular) style are fakes. They have stiff strokes and edges. Yongle wares have misty and hazy washes.

The hand-pressing cup, the underglazed red stem cup and the sweet-white bowl of the Yongle period are marked "made in Yongle reign". The characters are in a double circle, in a ball between two lions, or in flower scrolls framed by a circle.

Only in the Xuande period was the reign mark for official wares widely used. More prominent, it has six characters (rarely four) in the regular style or occasionally in seal script. Instead of being only on the base, it can appear elsewhere - in the interior, on their shoulders or under the mouth rim, horizontally or vertically.

A Xuande green-glaze dish with flower.

明初宣德**青釉花式盤**。

A Yongle blue-and-white straight-mouth bowl without base mark.

明代永樂**青花**
「**一把蓮**」**直口盤**(無底款)

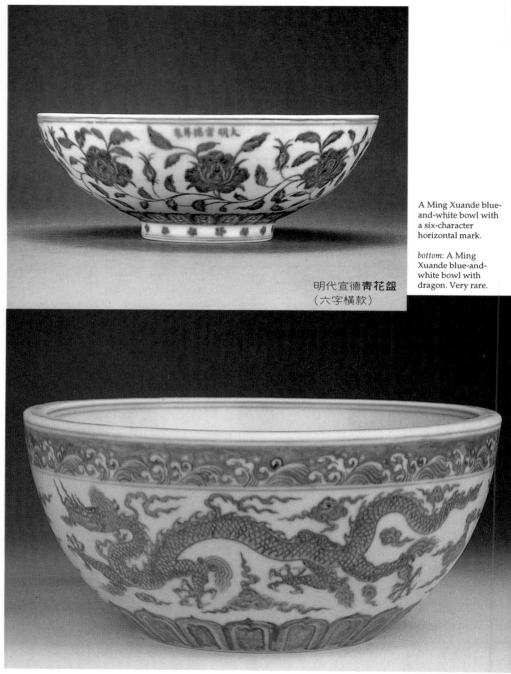

A Ming Xuande blue-and-white bowl with a six-character horizontal mark.

bottom: A Ming Xuande blue-and-white bowl with dragon. Very rare.

明代宣德**青花盌**
（六字橫款）

明代宣德**青花龍紋缸**，極珍罕。

48

Fallibility of Partial Evidence

A friend who likes Xuande official wares bought an inexpensive large bowl, thinking it was a genuine Xuande blue-and-white. However, from the reign mark, motif and glaze, I found it to be an imitation from mid or late Qing. But, he argued, he had based his judgement on the fact that the stroke on top of *xin* (心) in the character *de* (德) is missing, a point many authenticators have agreed is indicator of a genuine item.

Such partial evidence is unreliable. Instead, carefully examine every part of the ware including the body, motif, form, reign mark and periodic style.

A closer examination reveals the stylistic difference. The *xin* in *de* is not as well-balanced as the *xin* on the original Xuande mark, and the first and second strokes for *de* are not slanted outwards, as is usually the case.

Also, the characters show uniformity in stroke size and consistency in colour. An original has uneven ink tone and hazy fringes on the characters due to its special cobalt blue pigment.

A straight-mouth blue-and-white
bowl with beautiful women.
Xuande with a six-character mark
within a double circle.

明代宣德青花美人直口盤
（六字雙圈款）

明成化**青花宮盌**。

A Chenghua blue-and-white court bowl.

The Vigour-Within-Softness Characteristic of Chenghua Mark

In authenticating ceramics, do not ignore the smaller components. One example is the reign mark on Chenghua (mid Ming) wares. The "made in Chenghua reign of Ming dynasty" marks are in the regular style. The characters in two rows are encircled by a double circle or double square. A few have the characters aligned horizontally or vertically in a single row.

The *tian* (sky) mark on the base of covered jars is another periodic feature of Chenghua mark. The use of spontaneous and simple calligraphy results in the well-known vigour-within-softness aesthetic quality.

Fakes lack the easy rhythmic brushwork of the originals.

Another trait of Chenghua mark is the proximity between characters. The blue-and-white marks have uneven washes and the characters have hazy, visible fringes when viewed under a 10X magnifying glass.

明代成化**青花盌**
（六字雙行雙圈款）

A blue-and-white bowl
with a six-character
mark within a double
circle. Ming dynasty,
Chenghua mark and
period.

明代正德**黃釉碟**，
六字雙行雙圈款。

A yellow-glaze dish
from the Zhengde
period with six
characters within a
double circle.

A yellow-ground blue-and-white
dish with floral petals. Ming
dynasty, Zhengde mark and
period within a double circle.

明正德**黃地青花折枝花**果紋盤，
「大明正德年製」雙圈款。

The Marks of Hongzhi and Zhengde Period

The blue-and-white pigment mark for Hongzhi wares usually has the six characters arranged in two columns. Sometimes it is written in two columns inside a double circle, in the regular *(kai)* calligraphic style - rarely in the seal style. Some yellow-glaze Hongzhi fakes had seal-style marks to create an antiquated Ming look but fail to pass as the originals.

The calligraphy of Chenghua marks is plain, elegant yet vigorous but Hongzhi marks are delicate and in the regular style.

By the Zhengde period, both porcelain and glaze had become thick, showing bubbles, but the reign mark that is consistently written in the regular style is compact and strictly composed.

明代弘治**甜白釉龍紋碟**
（六字雙行款）

A sweet-white glazed dish with dragon motif. Hongzhi mark with six characters in two columns.

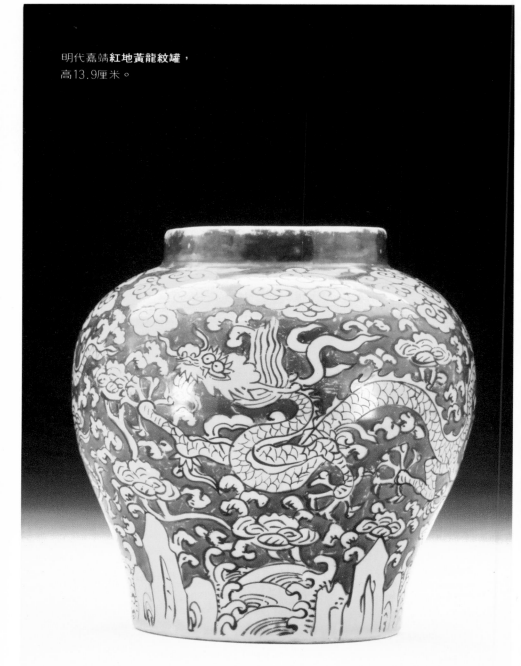

明代嘉靖**紅地黃龍紋罐**，
高13.9厘米。

A red-ground jar decorated with yellow dragon motif. Jiajing. H: 13.9cm.

The Marks of Late Ming Dynasty Wares

Marks on ceramics of the Jiajing period of Ming dynasty are varied. Some have auspicious characters like *fu shou kang ling* (fortune, longevity, health, peace) or *wan fu you tong* (abundant fortune for one and all). However, the three stages of the period have marks in different calligraphic style. Early Jiajing style is formal and structured, mid Jiajing contrived yet free-flowing, and late Jiajing, rough-brushed and heavy-toned.

The thick mark of the Longqing period appears in the six-character　大明隆慶年造　or *daming longqing nian zao* (literally, "made in Ming Longqing reign"). Fake wares often carry the character *zhi* (　製　) instead of *zao* (　造　).

Ceramics of these two periods are not worth collecting, even the official wares. There are few fine pieces and the heavy ones tend to look rough and clumsy with uneven glaze, imbalanced form and shoddy decoration.

Ceramics of the Wanli period of late Ming are mostly porous with disorderly motif and ill-painted figures. Marks of that period do not have *zao* but instead carry *zhi*.

明萬曆**五彩盌**（青花款，民窯）

left: A wucai blue-and-white bowl made in a private kiln. Ming dynasty, Wanli mark and period.

left: A Ming Wanli six-character mark in three columns inside a square frame (official ware).
明萬曆六字三行方框款（官窯）

明代嘉靖**青花三友花卉盤**

A blue-and-white bowl decorated with three types of flowers. Ming dynasty, Jiajing mark and of the period.

清代康熙鬥彩
十二花神盃——蘭花。

A doucai cup with orchids. Kangxi.

A pair of Kangxi doucai bowls. DM: 14.3cm. Very rare.

一對罕有的康熙鬥彩盌，
直徑14.3厘米。

The Marks of Kangxi Wares

Kangxi official wares like the Kang *wucai* and blue-and-white are cherished for their layered depictions of motifs. Imitations lack this and have lifeless and hazy motifs.

When buying Kangxi official wares, check not just the reign mark on the base but also the other parts for a more accurate authentication.

The most popular marks are those in blue-and-white pigment with heaped-and-piled effect. The character *kang* (康) is in regular calligraphic style while the strokes in *shui* (水) seem to stick together.

The four-character marks read *kangxi yi zhi* (康熙御製), the six-character marks, *daqing kangxi nian zhi* (大清康熙年製); those with the four-character marks are very fine wares. Fakes have these marks with stiff and lifeless strokes.

Kangxi porcelain pieces with reign marks of more than six characters are very rare.

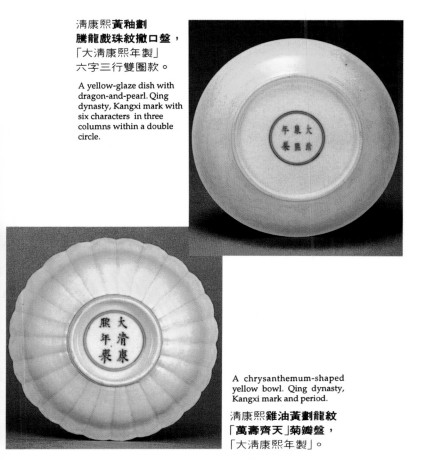

清康熙**黃釉劃**
騰龍戲珠紋撇口盤，
「大清康熙年製」
六字三行雙圈款。

A yellow-glaze dish with dragon-and-pearl. Qing dynasty, Kangxi mark with six characters in three columns within a double circle.

A chrysanthemum-shaped yellow bowl. Qing dynasty, Kangxi mark and period.

清康熙**雞油黃劃龍紋**
「**萬壽齊天」菊瓣盤，**
「大清康熙年製」。

清代雍正粉彩團花盌。

A fencai bowl with floral design.
Yongzheng.

A pair of fencai and doucai dishes
decorated with dragons. Qing dynasty,
Yongzheng mark.

清代雍正粉彩
鬥彩龍紋碟一對。

Features of Yongzheng Mark

Collectors of Yongzheng official wares know that the blue-and-white, *wucai* and *doucai* wares differ from the austere, thick pieces of the Kangxi reign. The *fencai* (famille rose) ware famous for its light, handsome form and splendid decoration, is identified by its body, glaze and decoration. The porcelain is very fine; even the base is smooth and shiny.

Yongzheng wares bear the reign mark on the base. The six-character *daqing yongzheng nian zhi* (大清雍正年製) or four-character *yongzheng nian zhi* (雍正年製) are in regular *(kai)* calligraphy. The seal style is rare and written vertically.

Some official wares have marks in other styles, like those on the base of opaque enamels, using cobalt blue, blue-and-white or copper red pigments. Early Yongzheng reign marks have shoddy calligraphy while those of the mid and later periods have delicate, well-composed, forceful and vigorous strokes. The calligraphy is usually in the Song regular style. The first stroke in (隹) is missing; while the character *zheng* (正) ends with a heavy stroke of thick ink. Fakes lack these traits.

清雍正**珊瑚紅地五彩牡丹紋盤，**
「雍正御製」雙方圈款。

A coral-red ground wucai bowl with peonies, Qing dynasty, Yongzheng mark in a double square.

A sky-blue glazed bowl. DM: 13.3cm. Qing dynasty, Yongzheng mark.

清雍正**天藍釉撇口盤**
直徑13.3厘米。
「大清雍正年製」
六字雙行雙框款。

清雍正六字
雙行雙圈款
A six-character Yongzheng mark in two columns framed by a double circle.

清乾隆青花蓮托
八吉祥壺形連蓋雙耳瓶，
「大清乾隆年製」
六字三行篆書款，高50厘米。

Absence of the Character *Zao* in Qing Dynasty Official Ware Mark

A friend bought a few porcelain pieces thinking they were Yongzheng official wares. When told they were fakes, he insisted: 'But they have the mark *yongzheng nian zao*' (literally, "made in Yongzheng reign").

When authenticating ceramics, do not just rely on the characters in the base mark. Recent fakes also have the characters Yongzheng but in different writing style and colour. The character *zao* (造) in two of my friend's porcelain wares reveal them as fakes.

After the Kangxi period, there were porcelain pieces with special imperial marks that no one could own unless they were gifts from the emperors. Only the character *zhi* (製) is used in the base mark for all Qing dynasty wares.

Two other pieces have base marks with a blurry colour tone - unlike official wares before Qianlong period which have a very solid and deep purple.

The official famille rose wares of the Yongzheng reign have *yongzheng yi zhi* (雍正御製) or *yongzheng nian zhi* (雍正年製) in cobalt pigment. The marks in the regular calligraphic style are in two rows in a double square.

清雍正**五彩花鳥紋撇口盌**，
「**大清雍正年製**」雙圈款。
A wucai bowl with birds and flowers. Qing dynasty, Yongzheng mark in a double circle.

清雍正**珊瑚紅地
留白九蝠壽字盤**，
口徑15.6厘米。
「**大清雍正年製**」
六字雙行雙圈款。

left : A blue-and-white lotus ewer with cover and design of eight auspicious emblems. Qing dynasty, Qianlong mark with six characters in three columns inscribed in seal style. H: 50cm.

A coral-red ground dish with nine auspicious bats. The base is white. DM: 15.6cm. Qing dynasty, Yongzheng mark with six characters in two columns within a double circle.

乾隆時民窰底款有「造」字。

Popular wares of the Qianlong period have the character "zao" in the base mark.

清乾隆**珊瑚紅地琺瑯彩盌**，六字三行篆書款。

A coral-red ground enamelled bowl. Qing dynasty, Qianlong mark with six characters in three columns in seal style.

The Seal Style Calligraphy Used in Qianlong Reign Mark

According to the book *Ceramic Elegance*, Yongzheng and Qianlong blue-and-white wares are incomparable to Kangxi's. Actually, porcelain pieces of the three reigns have distinctive features. I like the Kangxi blue-and-white as it is bright, splendid and layered. Qianlong wares have more variety, thick and dense colours although earlier ones have dispersed tones.

During Emperor Qianlong's 60-year reign, the quality of wares varied. Some blue-and-white made with thin paste were greyish dark.

The Qianlong reign mark can have six or four characters in a double square or circle. The calligraphy is seal *(zhuan)* style - squarish, well-balanced, orderly and elegant with even strokes.

In real Qianlong wares, the 丂 that is part of the character 令 is written as "s". In imitations, it looks like the figure "2".

In official wares, the top two strokes for the character *nian* (年) are apart, unlike in imitation or inferior popular wares.

Official wares of the Jiajing reign have neat marks; the popular wares have shoddy ones.

Some blue-and-white of the Daoguang reign are imitations of Ming Xuande but have uneven glaze, thick clay body and stiff motifs. *Fencai* wares marked with *Shendetang* (慎德堂) are better as they were used by the emperor.

The *fencai* wares of the Tongzhi period are inferior and have red marks in the regular style. However, the characters are well crafted.

清乾隆六字
雙行篆書款

A Qing dynasty
Qianlong reign mark
with six characters
in two columns, and
in the seal script.

清代乾隆**粉彩鏤空六方瓶**，高40.7厘米。

A fencai hexagonal vase in open-work. Qianlong. H: 40.7cm.

THE CHARACTERISTICS OF WARES OF EACH DYNASTY

Part II

清代乾隆**白料胎**
黃地鳳凰牡丹囊形尊，
高18.2厘米。
「乾隆年製」藍料款，
曾在蘇富比拍賣。

A yellow-ground pouch-shaped zun made of white body-material with phoenixes and peonies. Qing dynasty, Qianlong mark in blue pigment. H:18.2cm. Featured in one of Sotheby's auctions.

明代萬曆**綠地青龍罐**。

A green-ground jar with green dragon. Ming Wanli.

清代乾隆**釉裏紅葫蘆形花瓶**，高29.6厘米。

An underglazed red gourd-shaped vase. Qianlong. H: 29.6cm.

清代乾隆 **粉彩戲嬰雙耳瓶**。

A fencai double-handled vase with children at play. Qianlong.

明初洪武**釉裏紅花卉紋盌**，
呈色鮮艷，極罕。

An underglazed
red bowl with
flowers. Has a
rare intense red
colour. Hongwu
period, early
Ming dynasty.

元代**釉裏紅花斑玉壺春瓶**一對，高22厘米。
A pair of underglazed red yu hu chun vases with
floral specks. Yuan dynasty. H: 22cm.

70

UNDERGLAZED RED

The Early Underglazed Red Porcelain

The underglazed red ware was created by Jingdezhen in the Yuan dynasty. Often unmarked, they are hard to date. One clue is a 1338 jar, excavated from Jiangxi.

It is very difficult to make the red colour even and brilliant. The pigment is a copper red material from copper oxide. After the motif is painted, it is given a coat of transparent glaze. Then the ware is fired once at high temperature; hence the difficulty in controlling the colour. Although the white glaze has a hidden greenish tinge and is thick and brilliant, the glazed surface is unevenly toned, showing flint-stone red and metallic smudges due to the content of copper and iron. Imitations lack this feature which is often used to authenticate Yuan underglazed red ware.

Underglazed red wares of the Hongwu period, early Ming dynasty, also lack a pure red colour. Their motifs in flower and dragon-and-phoenix are fine and delicate. Yuan wares are simpler in thick ink.

An underglazed red vase decorated with enamel and a late Yuan underglazed red water spout.

元末**釉裏紅芭蕉紋水注**（右）
和**釉裏紅彩繪瓶**（左）。

元末明初（近洪武時期）
釉裏紅花卉紋瓶，
呈色鮮艷完整，
極罕，高32厘米。
（曾在蘇富比拍賣）

The Underglazed Red Wares of Yuan Dynasty Turn Black Easily

Common Yuan dynasty underglazed red wares are bowls, dishes and plates. There are a few vases, jars and stem cups. Jars with everted mouth-rims have the most elaborate designs, some with more than ten tiers of motifs.

The jars have mouths that are wider than their bases, and clear joints on the body, features useful in authentication.

Most of the pigments have turned black or grey, the red colour is not pure and the washes are uneven. This is due to the firing.

The colour for underglazed red comes from copper. Copper is unstable and decomposes at temperatures above 1,250° Celsius. If the pressure in the kiln is unstable during the reduction process, the copper will combine with the carbon and oxygen and turn into copper oxide, copper, copper carbonate or oxidized copper acid. Only the copper acid is red, hence the difficulty in control during the firing process.

The iron content in the body material must be very low to produce a white colour or a translucent greenish tone.

Motifs on the underglazed red ware are favourite traditional ink paintings.

元代**釉裏紅**
雙鳳紋平底盌,
直徑十三厘米。
An underglazed red
flat-based bowl with a
pair of phoenixes.
Yuan dynasty.
DM: 13cm.

left: An underglazed red vase with floral design, in bright colour and perfect condition, very rare. H: 32cm. Late Yuan - early Ming, Hongwu. Featured in one of Sotheby's auctions.

明代洪武**釉裏紅花卉盌**，罕有。
直徑廿一厘米，約值港幣二百萬元。
A rare underglazed bowl with flowers. Hongwu.
DM: 21cm. Worth approximately HK$2 million.

The Underglazed Red of Ming and Early Qing Dynasties

Very few underglazed red wares were produced in the Hongwu period of the Ming dynasty. A Sotheby's auction held in Hong Kong, 1989, sold a large Hongwu bowl with peonies and chrysanthemums. The price was HK$18.5 million - an indication of the value of such porcelain.

By the Xuande period of the Ming dynasty, the quality of the porcelain had improved greatly. The red became bright and fresh with the correct intensity and this contrasted beautifully with the orange-peel motif of the white glaze. Wares of the Chenghua period are also intense and brilliant, but there are only a few of these.

By the Hongzhi and Zhengde periods, underglazed red had become scarce and were too red or greyish.

Kangxi and Yongzheng underglazed red are mainly imitations of Xuande official wares. Bright with clear motifs and finely incised lines, they are also known as *bao shao hong* (treasured red) during the Yongzheng reign.

Fakes have emerged in Taiwan recently but they have a shimmer on the surface.

清初康熙**釉裏紅**
罕有水盂。

An underglazed red water jar. Kangxi.

清乾隆青花釉裏紅
雲海游龍大天球瓶，
高48.5厘米，罕有。
「大清乾隆年製」
六字三行篆書款
（曾在蘇富比拍賣）。

76

Difficulty in Producing Underglazed Blue-and-Red Ware

The magnificent underglazed blue-and-red ceramics result from the perfect fusion of the blue pigment of blue-and-white and the red pigment of underglazed red.

Production started in the Yuan dynasty and ceased in the early Ming dynasty. Revived in the Xuande period of the Ming dynasty, it was named the blue-and-white with aubergine ware and has a brilliant red glaze.

It became scarce after the Chenghua period and the most valuable are those of the Xuande period. It was not until the Kangxi period of the Qing dynasty that superior pieces resurfaced.

Most Yongzheng underglazed blue-and-red wares have glazes with orange-peel cracks and rich, lively decorations. There are uneven washes in the blue-and-white section of the glaze, while the underglazed red section is lighted painted. In inferior pieces, the red has turned blackish brown.

Qianlong underglazed blue-and-red have a more stable red.

An underglazed blue-and-red vase with "three winter friends" (left); another with dragon-and-cloud. Qianlong.

清代乾隆
青花釉裏紅膽瓶
「歲寒三友」(左)
和「雲龍」(右)。

left: A large globular underglazed blue-and-red with a dragon frolicking amidst clouds. H: 48.5cm. Very rare. Qing dynasty, Qianlong reign mark with six characters in three columns. Seal script calligraphy. Featured in one of Sotheby's auctions.

元朝青花人物玉壶春瓶，
高24.9厘米。

BLUE-AND-WHITE WARE

The Blue-and-White Ware Dating from Yuan Dynasty to Early Ming Dynasty

Yuan blue-and-white are usually big, thick in body, heavy and whitish. Motifs are painted freehand, multi-layered, elaborate but orderly.

Low manganese, high iron content and arsenic in the imported cobalt led to a brilliant, intense colour with black specks on the surface.

Early Ming wares have scattered motifs and a subtly greyish colour.

During the Yongle and Xuande periods, blue-and-white flourished. Better techniques on body and glaze production made available fine, white biscuit and brilliant, translucent glazes.

left: A yu hu chun vase with figure. Yuan dynasty. H: 24.9cm.

明代洪武青花
纏枝紋棱口盃托

A lobed blue-and-white dish with flowers. Hongwu, Ming dynasty.

元代青花罐
（唐太宗故事）

A blue-and-white jar, Yuan, depicting a story of Emperor Tang Taizong.

79

明初永樂**青花蓮子盌**，
直徑10厘米，
曾在太古佳士得拍賣。

The Authentication of Blue-and-White Ware of Yongle Period

The thin glazed wares of the Yongle period of the Ming dynasty is one of the prototypes of porcelain in succeeding dynasties.

Porcelain of the Yongle and Xuande periods used a foreign pigment, *Sulimani*, to improve the quality of the blue-and-white pigment. Due to *Sulimani*, Yongle wares have translucent and clear glazes painted with refreshing floral and tree motifs. Animals and figures are rare as *Sulimani* produces uneven washes. *Sulimani* black specks are important to the identification of ceramic style. Another clue is the smaller floral scrolls on Yuan wares, and the small leaves but large flowers on Yongle wares.

The unique fringe decorative pattern of dotted flower, Islamic motif and curly grass was inherited from the blue-and-white of the Xuande period. Yongle wares also have painting on the core of the vessel.

明代永樂**青花扁壺**。

A blue-and-white bian vase. Yongle.

A blue-and-white bowl with peach blossom on inner wall. Yongle. Worth approximately HK\$4.5 million. Very rare.

明代永樂**青花盌**(內壁壽桃花紋圖案)，約值四百五十萬港元，罕有。

明初宣德**青花龍紋梅瓶**，高45厘米，珍罕。

The Glazes of Blue-and-White Ware of Xuande Period

The blue-and-white ware of the Xuande period is cherished for its tone and charm. The wide range of colour is due to the three types of cobalt blue material.

The first pigment, *Sulimani*, leaves blackish brown specks on the body but has a stable colour with depth.

The second is a mixture of *Sulimani* and native cobalt. This has the right intensity of colour tone and clearly layered motifs.

The third is mainly native cobalt which produces a glaze that tends to run and an unstable, pale tone. The blue-and-white official ware of the early Xuande period is highly valued. The later ones, darker with specks or pale grey without specks, are inferior.

The orange-peel glaze is unique to Xuande blue-and-white. Such ware has a thick, white glaze filled with bubbles - the bubbles have surfaced and cracked during the firing process, forming little dents or needle eyes on the glaze surface.

The whiteware among Xuande blue-and-white is a translucent, pale green due to the oxidized iron.

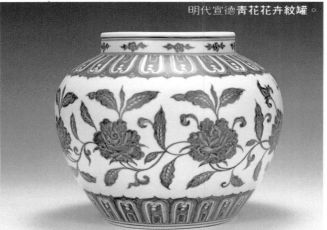

明代宣德青花花卉紋罐。

A blue-and-white jar with flowers. Ming dynasty, Xuande.

left: A blue-and-white mei ping vase with dragon. Ming dynasty, Xuande. H: 45cm. Very rare.

A blue-and-whiite stem cup with dragon. Xuande.

明代宣德
青花龍紋高足盌

83

Views of
blue-and-
white stem
cup with
nine
dragons.
Xuande.

明代宣德青花
九龍紋高足盌（兩面）

84

The Blue-and-White Stem Cups of Xuande Period

I recall a blue-and-white stem cup of the Xuande period in the British Museum. It stood out with its pattern of sea waves and four dragons. A fifth dragon was on its stem.

The period boasts a rich variety of stem cups, including the ten-lobed stem cup and stem cups with hollow cores.

They come in various sizes and designs, including one with a solid base. Typical motifs are dragons, figures and floral scrolls. Besides the blue-and-white, there is also the underglazed red ware with three fish (symbolizing abundance) and three fruits.

The dragon is the favourite motif. There are the sea dragon, dragon in the clouds, and winding dragon amongst others.

Some memorable Xuande stem cups have an "empty space" *(liu bai)* style, giving a feeling of of depth.

Superior Xuande blue-and-white have thin and even glazes. They also have minute bubbles and needle eyes on the surface. Their white powder-like feature is special.

A blue-and-white ground stem cup
with dragon. Xuande.

明代宣德**藍地空白花**
波濤海獸高足盌

清代雍正青花
纏枝花卉壺形雙耳尊
（高33.5厘米）

86

The Blue-and-White Ware of Early Qing Dynasty

The dragon is a cultural symbol of China. Thus, the early Qing blue-and-white ware with dragons is a favourite among collectors in Hong Kong.

The blue-and-white of the Kangxi period have clear tonal variations and their decorations are multi-layered, with figures predominating.

Yongzheng *doucai* and *fencai* wares are unique but the blue-and-white generally cannot match those of the Kangxi period. In fact, many are imitations.

In terms of aesthetic value, Yongzheng wares fall behind those of the Ming dynasty.

The blue-and-white motifs on Kangxi wares are refined and exquisite. Imitations lack layers and have lifeless motifs.

As far as clay body is concerned, Yongzheng and Qianlong wares are not as thick and compact as Kangxi wares. Their imitations are so porous and light that a collector can actually "feel" one.

The blue-and-white wares of Yongzheng period have light bodies and thin glazes. The large pieces are well-balanced but not heavy. However, they lack the artistry of the cream of Kangxi wares.

left: A blue-and-white zun with two handles decorated with floral scroll. Qing dynasty, Yongzheng. H: 33.5cm.

清康熙**青花八仙盌**。

A blue-and-white bowl decorated with eight deities. Qing dynasty, Kangxi.

A blue-and-white cup with pomegranate. Qing dynasty, Kangxi mark with six characters in two columns.

清康熙**青花**
石榴花題詩花神盃，
「大清康熙年製」六字二行款。

87

A blue-and-white bowl with hexagrams and sea waves. Qing dynasty, Kangxi mark.

清康熙青花
八卦海濤紋盌
「大清康熙年製

A blue-and-white bowl with everted rim decorated with floral scroll. Qing dynasty, Kangxi mark in double circle.

清代康熙青花纏枝
蓮紋撇口盌（雙圈款）

The Solid and Fine Glaze of Blue-and-White Ware of Kangxi Period

The blue-and-white vases of the Kangxi period are my favourite. Their elegance and quiet charm is enhanced by their multi-layered tones. It is no wonder that the Qing dynasty writer, Chen Liu, in *Ceramic Elegance* said that the world's best ceramics are in China while China's best ceramics are the Kangxi wares.

Kangxi blue-and-white have excellent craftsmanship. The official wares especially have a perfect fusion of body and glaze. The cobalt blue pigment has varied tones and is thus able to reflect different shades. It has an oxidized cobalt content of only about three to five percent. As it is an underglaze colour, it is resistant to scratches, pollution and fading.

The tonal quality of the Kangxi official ware reached its height with the *zhu ming* (珠明) and *zhe* (浙) material. Some well-known blue-and-white pieces are emerald feather blue and sapphire blue.

Kangxi wares fall roughly into three periods. The early pieces have a greyish and darker tone. Those in the middle period are a lovely jade-green with the glaze turning from off green to white. They are heavier and thicker. In late Kangxi, the glaze is pure and lustrous. Ceramic art had reached its peak.

清康熙**青花瓜果紋小碟**，
「大清康熙年製」
六字二行雙圈款。
A blue-and-white saucer with melons. Qing dynasty, Kangxi mark in six characters inside a double circle.

A blue-and-white bowl with children and lady. Qing dynasty, Kangxi.

清代康熙**青花仕女童子執桂瓷盌**。

清代雍正青花松竹梅紋壺。

A blue-and-white vase with pine, plum and bamboo. Qing dynasty, Yongzheng.

The Exquisite and Elegant Blue-and-White Ware of Yongzheng Period

Blue-and-white porcelain reached its zenith during the Kangxi to Yongzheng period. Early Qianlong wares had inherited the fine tradition of the Yongzheng reign, making them valuable collectibles.

However, the late Qianlong blue-and-white suffered a decline in artistry with shoddy craftsmanship, stiff motifs and overworked patterns. They thus lack the value of Yongzheng official wares, noted for their fine porcelain body, elegant decoration and balanced profile.

Most people think that Yongzheng blue-and-white ware is mainly an imitation of Ming blue-and-white. Actually, the former can be categorized as:

1. Imitation of wares of the Yongle and the Xuande periods.
2. Imitation of wares of the Jiajing period.
3. The original type of the Yongzheng period.

The second category has lively and vigorous pieces but is largely unheeded as it is not representative of Yongzheng blue-and-white.

In the first category are wares attempting the natural washes and metallic smudges of the Ming. The imitations of Xuande blue-and-white, especially, have a deep blue but an unstable colour with a faint greenish tinge on the fringe of the motif and metallic smudges on the thickly coloured parts.

The Yongzheng blue-and-white wares have depth of colour after dotting, but the colour floats, making it less valuable than Xuande wares. Their orange-peel effect and flint-stone red are less fluid and lack rhythm. The popular wares are rather crude.

The special blue-and-white material on the period ware came from the cobalt mines in Shaoxing and Jinhua, Zhejiang province.

The motifs, detailed figures and flowers are inspired by the fine-lined painting style.

清雍正鬥彩竹枝盌，
口徑9.3厘米，
「大清雍正年製」款。

A doucai bowl with bamboo.
Yongzheng. DM:9.3cm. Qing
dynasty, Yongzheng mark.

清代乾隆年製苹有
鬥彩三多紋扁壺
高31.8厘米。

Official Wares of Early Qianlong Period Make Top Choice

Porcelain experts acknowledge the superb quality of early Qianlong wares. They have a fine biscuit, well-balanced shape, elaborate motif and neat joint at the foot ring.

However, in the later period, lifeless designs, poor pictorial composition and over-worked motifs led to a decline in quality. This was especially seen in the blue-and-white, *doucai, fencai* and iron-red wares.

Another factor was an over-emphasis on auspicious emblems like *fu lu shou* (literally, "fortune, emolument and longevity") and *ru yi ji xiang* (literally, "good luck and fortune"). Overused characters like these made the porcelain appear vulgar. In addition, some motifs were contrived, congested and repetitive.

The writer prefers the early pieces, which are mostly marked wth a six-character seal script calligraphy reign mark. It is good to note that the characters *nian* and *zhi* are written in the same style as that on the mark of late Yongzheng porcelain.

Actually, since mid Qianlong reign, official wares have begun to move towards realism, with much dotting, shading and thick two-dimensional shading.

Wares of late Qianlong have uneven thickness. Even among official wares, there are some with cracked glaze.

It is important to be selective in picking porcelain from the Qianlong reign. Often, you can judge one by touching and feeling the smoothness of the body, the glaze of the ware, and checking the base of the foot ring for rough edges.

left: A rare bianhu flask decorated in doucai with san duo (three kinds of fruit symbolizing abundance). Qianlong. H:31.8cm.

清乾隆青花番蓮
「萬壽無疆」撇口盌一對，
「大清乾隆年製」篆書款。

A pair of blue-and-white bowls with everted rim decorated with lotus scrolls and four characters "wan shou wu jiang" to denote longevity. Qing dynasty, Qianlong mark (seal script) and of the period.

A blue-and-white vase with a garlic-shaped mouth decorated with petals of flowers. Qing dynasty, Qianlong mark and period.

The Tone of Blue-and-White Ware of Qianlong Period

The colour of the blue-and white ware of the Qianlong period has often been thought to be only a deep and dense blue. Actually, the tone has undergone some changes.

The early pieces have unstable colour, producing uneven washes at the edges of the motifs. Pieces from the final years of the period have a bright tone that is stable and visually harmonious.

Imitations of Qianlong wares produced in the early Republic tend to be coloured too thickly with motifs which are not well-layered. The colour tone seems diluted and dispersed, making the painting less attractive.

The blue-and-white of late Qianlong are tinged with a greyish tone but are still quite deeply coloured. A few pieces from mid Qianlong display motifs amidst mixed layers of shade with a blackish tinge. These are, at most, second-rate wares.

清代乾隆**青花天球大瓶**。

A blue-and-white globular vase. Qianlong.

A blue-and-white oblong-shaped bowl with floral scrolls. Qianlong.

清乾隆**青花長方水仙盆**。

清乾隆青花
折枝番蓮紋壺形貫耳六方瓶，
高45.2厘米，「大清乾隆年製」
六字三行篆書款。

96

Paintings on Official Wares

To appreciate the official wares of the Ming and Qing dynasties, I touch the porcelain to feel its smoothness. I also pay attention to the subject and painting style of the motif as both are closely related to the painting style of the period - an important aspect in authentication.

Many blue-and-white and *doucai* wares of the Yongzheng period used the technique of ink painting of that period. The fruit motif was inspired by the "Four King Painters" of the Yuan dynasty. Especially appealing are the floral paintings which were greatly influenced by famous artists like Yun Nantian.

Yun Nantian's brushwork is charming, elegant and free-flowing. His painting style originated from the boneless method and his works evoke a misty atmosphere. He inspired the common motifs of lotus, peony, peach and chrysanthemum.

In the Qianlong period, the motifs on early official pieces emphasized the expressive style which, by mid Qianlong, had turned towards the realistic.

Wares made before the Qianlong period had a brilliance and an enhanced dimensional quality in the paintings. This was due to the halo light and colourful haze. Poetry and verses embellished the paintings.

Official wares of late and mid Qianlong period had motifs in various ink painting techniques like the two-dimensional colouring, dotting, *chun* (rubbing) and shading.

Paintings on mid Qianlong wares carry romantic charm and artistic themes. They later deteriorated as overuse of the fine-line *(gong bi)* method rendered the motifs artificial, repetitive and stiff. The flaw is especially obvious on blue-and-white and *doucai* wares. Official wares of the preceding Yongzheng period boast finer paintings of flowers and figures.

A doucai bowl decorated with floral design. Yongzheng. Six-character mark in double circle and the regular style of calligraphy.

清雍正鬥彩團花盌，
雙圈雙行六字楷書款。

left: A blue-and-white hexagonal vase with handles and decorated with floral petals. Qing dynasty, Qianlong. H: 45.2cm. Six-character, three-column mark in seal script.

97

The Decline of Blue-and-White Wares of Jiaqing Period

Among the blue-and-white of the Jiaqing period, the earlier pieces (nearer to the Qianlong period) are superior and yet are generally cheaper than Qianlong wares. The similarity in form and motif between wares of both periods may confuse novice collectors. But a careful look will reveal that Jiaqing porcelain wares lack the proportion, fineness and charm of Qianlong wares and have a deeper but not necessarily cleaner glaze.

The enamelled pieces and blue-and-white of the late Jiaqing period have a rough body, hazy colour and shoddy craftsmanship. This marked the point in the decline of Qing porcelain art. The reason is partly economic, the country being poor. During the Daoguang and Tongzhi periods, austerity ruled, hence the simplicity and shoddiness of porcelain pieces.

A blue-and-white yu hu chun vase. Early Jiaqing, Qing dynasty.

清代嘉慶初期
青花玉壺春瓶

清代嘉慶**青花梅瓶**

A blue-and-white mei ping. Jiaqing.

Fine Pieces are Rare Among Wares of Daoguang Period

I personally do not favour wares made after the Qianlong and Jiaqing periods. Imitations were abundant among popular wares of the Guangxu period; official wares, too, had little to offer. Wares of these periods are not worth collecting and investing in, although there is no harm in buying a couple of reasonably priced ones for your own enjoyment.

It is difficult to find exquisite porcelain that are similar to porcelain of the Kangxi, Yongzheng and Qianlong periods in the Daoguang period because of the decline in the country's economy.

Among Daoguang wares, the worthy collectibles are the yellow-glaze vessels in imitation of ivory and some gilt vessels decorated with red-streaked gilt design.

Late Daoguang saw wares that are thick, clumsy and porous with uneven shape. Some poor-quality wares, although named xuan ware（宣窰）or xuan green（宣青）are in essence products of the Daoguang period. Most of Daoguang wares do not show perfect fusion between body and glaze, except for *fencai* wares marked with *"Shendetang"*. These are porcelain used by Emperor Daoguang in his palace but few of them survived. Do beware of fakes of this type.

A blue-and-white bowl. Daoguang, Qing dynasty. Mark by Wen Langshan.

清代道光**青花盌**
（文朗珊款）

清道光**青花高足壺**
A blue-and-white stem pot.
Daoguang.

A blue-and-white bowl decorated with dragon and clouds. Daoguang.

清道光**青花**
雲龍紋直口盌

99

清代雍正**胭脂水雀盃**全套五件。

A set of five rouge-glazed waterpots. Yongzheng.

清代道光**胭脂水**(右)與**金玉彩小雀瓶**。

A gilt enamelled waterpot and a rouge-glazed waterpot. Daoguang.

The Blue-and-White Waterpots of Qing Dynasty

As collectibles, waterpots rarely come in a set. Even fine pairs are quite rare. A whole set consists of four pots and a small vase; most existing sets have no vase.

Often, when a whole set is available, one or two pieces are warped or cracked. To match them with a new pot means an uneven tone in the porcelain. Unavoidable changes in colour have arisen due to the wares changing hands and varying light conditions (including exposure to sunlight.)

Fine wares here include the rare and famous Yongzheng rouge-glazed waterpots (Daoguang period) and other blue-and-white sets such as those with the legendary motifs of "Sanniang Teaching Her Son" (三娘教子) and "The Seven Eccentrics of the Bamboo Forest" (竹林七賢). The chess-piece-shaped and the pointed-shaped pieces are among the sets. Some of them have additional decorative appeal because they have ice cracks under the glaze, a result of the firing process.

The blue-and-white waterpots of the Kangxi reign have the most brilliant colour. Official wares have dragon-and-phoenix, pine-and-bamboo, and flowers as the main motifs while legendary figures such as the Eight Deities (八仙) and *Romance of the Western Chamber* (西廂記) are found on the popular wares.

The blue-and-white waterpots of the Yongzheng period show a deep and intense blue with vigorous brushwork, which may be blackish blue, pale blue and hazy blue. Those on the market are mainly from the Guangxu period and early Republic, and are inferior to Kangxi and Yongzheng waterpots.

清代青花「三娘教子」雀盃全套五件。

A set of five blue-and-white waterpots decorated with "Sanniang Teaching Her Son". Qing dynasty.

101

A doucai covered jar with celestial
horse and "tian" character mark.
Very rare. H:11.3cm.

明代成化鬥彩飛馬蓋罐，
「天」字款，罕有，
高11.3厘米。

COLOURED GLAZES

Wucai and *Doucai* Wares of Chenghua Period

Chenghua official blue-and-white are noted for their elegance and freshness, though some of them are greyish-brown because of the native cobalt material.

Wucai ware top the list of Chenghua official wares with a subtly elegant tone and a sensuous contour even though only a few exist. They have a good colour, pure and fine biscuit and unusual motifs. Thus, according to *The Record of Porcelain*: '*Wucai* ware are the highest grade among Chenghua porcelain.'

Freedom from the constraints of cost enabled Chenghua potters to concern themselves with skill and artistry, creating some of the finest porcelain. The most famous coloured ware is the *doucai*, which combines blue with overglazed colours. This innovation influenced successive generations of porcelain.

The motif is first outlined on the clay body with blue-and-white glaze. Colours are added after firing; a second firing is done at a low temperature. Original Chenghua *doucai* pieces have a luxuriant, translucent appeal while their imitations show a floating gloss and weak brushwork.

明代成化
鬥彩花鳥高足盃，
高7.8厘米。

The character "tian" in the reign mark of a Chenghua jar.
明成化「**天**」**字罐**
的「天」款。

A doucai stem cup decorated with bird-and-flower. Chenghua.
H: 7.8cm.

明代成化**鬥彩雞盃，**
口徑8.2厘米。

A doucai chicken bowl.
Chenghua.
DM: 8.2cm.

明代弘治**雞油**
黃釉大碟，
六字雙行款。

A chicken-oil yellow-glaze
large plate with a six-character
mark inside a double circle.
Ming dynasty, Hongzhi mark
and period.

Yellow-Glaze Porcelain of Hongzhi Period

Most collectors of Ming dynasty porcelain concentrate on Yongle, Xuande and Chenghua wares, paying scant attention to those of the Hongzhi period. This is because Hongzhi ware is basically a continuation of Chenghua's; its blue-and-white pieces are similar to Chenghua pieces in colour tone and motif.

Many Hongzhi wares are dishes and bowls. The period's overglazed *wucai*, for example, is at most a shadow of Chenghua wares. The firing technique failed to match that of the Chenghua period and the quality continued to deteriorate.

However, the uniqueness of the yellow-glaze wares of the Hongzhi period make them worthwhile collecting. Luxurious pieces with a fresh yellow colour fetch the highest prices.

As the imperial kilns of the period were closed for 18 consecutive years, production was limited; besides, there were more pure-white porcelain and very few pieces with coloured glaze.

Hongzhi yellow-glaze ware was reputed to be the best. It had reached the highest standard of low-temperature yellow-glaze porcelain and represented the peak of this ceramic type. There were already a few pieces of yellow-glaze porcelain in the Chenghua period but they were experimental wares.

The pure yellow-glaze wares were produced by sprinkling the glaze onto the porcelain body, hence it is also called *jiao* (sprinkle) *huang* (yellow). The end product is bright and translucent, reflecting details of the incised motifs. Its soft, pale tone distinguished it from the deep yellow glazes of the Jiajing and Wanli periods.

A yellow-glaze blue-and-white
bowl with fruit. Hongzhi.

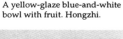

明代弘治**黃釉青花果盤**

Yellow-Glaze Porcelain of Ming and Qing Dynasties

Collectors of Qing porcelain like wares of the Yongzheng period. Besides the famous *fencai*, blue-and-white and *wucai*, the other outstanding group is the sky green with its lasting appeal.

The period's "powdered green" and "plum green" imitation of Longquan ware are a match for ware of the Yongle period. They are vigorous and elegant. The *ji hong* (clear red) ware that come in small cups , vases and dishes are also beautiful.

Then, there are the lovely yellow-glaze porcelain bowls and plates. Iron is a colourant in this ceramic and it is known as "iron yellow"; but the yellow glaze of Yongzheng *fencai* used oxidized antimony as a colourant and is thus called "antimony yellow".

Yellow glaze originated from the Xuande period, reaching a high technical level during the Chenghua and Hongzhi periods.

The pure yellow-glaze bowls, cups and dishes inherited the ceramic tradition of the Hongzhi period; their pigment is ochre which has a higher content of iron. New names, " chicken-oil yellow" and "egg-yolk yellow" indicate the different shades of the glaze.

清康熙**黃釉劃圍花
雲頭紋直口盌**
「大清康熙年製」
六字二行雙圈款。
A yellow-glaze bowl with
flowers and clouds. Qing
dynasty, Kangxi mark and
period in six characters
inside a double circle.

A yellow-glaze vase with
two handles and lotus
scrolls. Daoguang.

清代道光**黃釉
刻纏枝蓮雙耳瓶**

Wucai Ware of Kangxi Period Display a Clam Light

A seasoned collector of official wares know that fine pieces are not cheap. Therefore he would be aware of the many cheap *wucai* fakes (mainly popular wares).These fakes lack a firm body, fluent brushwork and a thin layer of light on the glaze. Top choice among Kangxi *wucai* ware are those from the Lang kiln, which surpass similar ones from the Ming.

Wucai ware existed in the late Ming dynasty. It is a mixture of overglazed polychrome and underglazed blue-and-white enamel.

The *wucai* wares of the Kangxi period are cherished for their solid body, pure and lustrous glaze. During the period, there was a breakthrough in polychrome decoration with a new type of ware decorated with overglazed blue enamel and shiny black enamel. Sometimes, even gold was added to *wucai*.

The lustre and rich contrasting hues of Kangxi *wucai* is attributed to the appropriate control of temperature in the kiln. Kangxi *wucai* pieces are often decorated in ochre, with details of flowers, leaves and folds of clothing of figures displaying tonal gradation and layering effect. This is a major difference from the one-dimensional painting technique of the Ming potters.

Because decorations for *wucai* stressed energetic brushwork, the result is an appearance of hardness and so, it is also known as *yingcai* (hard-colour ware); its glaze is hard and shows a clam light when examined from the side. It was fired at a temperature higher than that for *fencai* and is also called *gucai* (archaic-colour glaze).

清代康熙**五彩十二花神盃**一套，高5厘米。

A set of 12 wucai cups with flowers. Kangxi. H: 5cm.

An imperial fencai vase with bird-and-flower. Qing dynasty, Yongzheng blue-colour mark. Very rare. Worth HK$10 million.

清康熙**五彩果鳥盌**，
口徑20.3厘米。

A wucai bowl with bird-and-fruit. Kangxi. DM:20.3cm.

清康熙**五彩
龍鳳紋撇口盌**，
口徑10.5厘米。

A wucai bowl with everted rim. Decorated with dragon-and-phoenix. Kangxi. DM: 10.5cm.

清代雍正**粉彩花鳥紋罐**一對。
A pair of fencai jars with bird-and-flower.
Yongzheng.

The Three-Dimensional Effect of *Fencai* Ware

Recently, I chanced upon some *fencai* ware of the Tongzhi period which, the seller claimed, were Yongzheng's. A discerning collector will not be easily tricked.

Fencai porcelain of the Yongzheng period (especially official wares) have fine motifs, lustrous glaze, elegant pale colour and a strong three-dimensional effect.

Mr Geng Baochang commented: 'When inspected from the side, a faint colourful halo of light appears on the fringe of the painted motif which is set off by the white glaze.' This is an important point in authentication.

Fakes of the late Qing and early Republic have porous clay, imperfect fusion of clay and glaze, and shoddy craftsmanship.

Fencai, an overglazed enamel is painted on the fired body decorated with pure-white glaze. By the Qianlong period, coloured enamels like yellow, green, rouge red and gold were added to paint the ground.

清代雍正**粉彩**
梅竹靈芝紋大盤，罕有。

A large fencai dish with plum, bamboo and lingzhi fungus. Yongzheng. Very rare.

Fencai wares first appeared in the late Kangxi period and flourished in the Yongzheng period. It has a softer hue than Kangxi *wucai* and is also called soft-coloured ware.

Qianlong *fencai* ware contains lead, has a pale colour and rough glaze. Its motifs are elaborate, toned and coloured, with rouge-red flowers on contoured stalks.

貴重精巧的**粉彩小花瓶**，
清乾隆年製，
高19.1厘米（7½吋）。
An exquisite small fencai vase. Qing dynasty, Qianlong mark and period. H:19.1cm.

The Porcelain in Opaque Enamels of Early Qing Dynasty

Besides the famous *wucai* and blue-and-white Kangxi wares, a third category, porcelain in opaque enamels *or falangcai* (琺瑯彩), ranked among the period's finest.

In *falangcai*, coloured enamelled motifs are painted on plain biscuit which are then fired in the kiln. An overglazed ware, *falangcai* is also known as porcelain-painted enamelled ware.

Falangcai has a fine, translucent body and a handsome form. Combined with charming painting and bright colours, it is outstanding.

Kangxi *falangcai* was technically superb as the white-glazed biscuit was first fired at the official kilns in Jingdezhen, Jiangxi, and then sent to the court painters. The style was those of masters like the Four Wang's (四王) and Wu Hu (吳惲) and featured landscapes and bird-and-flower.

Imported colour pigments were mainly used for the decorations, with some native ochre and *doucai* pigments. These thick materials created a three-dimensional effect on the motifs.

清代雍正**琺瑯**「飛鳴宿食」盌，畫工完美。

The ware of the late Kangxi period was an imitation of the copper painted enamelled ware in colour. It was then mixed with the hard painting technique of the Ming dynasty, hence the archaic tone with thick body and patterned motifs.

By the Yongzheng period, paintings on porcelain were mere copies without the colour-filling technique of the Kangxi period. Wares were painted in soft colours on thin bodies. By the Qianlong period, the subjects were mainly Western figures and ancient patterns, marking a decline of famille rose.

A bowl in opaque enamels decorated with exquisitely painted birds and flowers. Yongzheng.

112

Fencai Revolving Vase of Qianlong Period

The revolving vase was first created in the late Qianlong period. It took different shapes and sizes. The body, inner core and base are separately fired and then luted.

The inner vase and the vase neck are luted and slid into the belly of the vase. The base is sealed, and holes are made on the belly so that the motifs on the revolving inner vase can be viewed from outside. Both the *zhuan xin ping* (revolving core vase) and the *zhuan jing ping* (revolving neck vase) were new from the Qianlong period and mainly in *fencai* wares.

Some impressive Qianlong revolving vases included a blue-glaze, gold-streaked *fencai* vase and one with a revolving core to hold water. Another well-known kind is the magnificent enamelled ware with design of a set of heavenly stems and earthly branches. The basic luting is similar for *zhuan xin ping* and *zhuan jing ping*, except that the latter has revolving rings on the neck. The heavenly stems are painted on the neck and the earthly branches on the body of the *zhuan jing ping*. Together, they form an amazing complete ten-thousand-year calendar!

乾隆**粉彩鏤空**
雲龍轉心瓷瓶 A fencai revolving vase (zhuan xin ping) decorated with open-work motif of cloud-and-dragon. Qianlong.

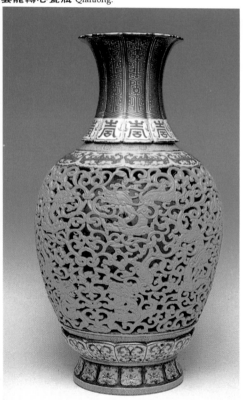

A gourd-shaped fencai revolving vase (zhuan xin ping) decorated with open-work on the interior with blue-and-white glaze. Qing. 乾隆**粉彩鏤空**
葫蘆式內青花轉心瓶。

Enamelled Wares of Guangzhou Marry Oriental and Western Art

Fine antique porcelain did not only come from the Jingdezhen area of Jiangxi province. There were also enamelled whiteware *(guangcai)* of Guangzhou.

Originating from the Yongzheng period, *guangcai* was initially meant for export. Production of the ware reached its highest level in the Qianlong and Jiaqing periods. Yongzheng *guangcai* ware is the rarest.

Created at a time when the *fencai* ware was blossoming, early *guangcai* wares were strongly influenced by *fencai*. By the Qianlong period, its light-toned decorations became more colourful and grand with tonal gradation. It also featured the structured, symmetrical gilt-panelled painting style of the Ming dynasty, using gold as the main colour complemented by red and green.

The porcelain of the Qianlong *guangcai* ware is thin and the glaze white and translucent; some pieces have characters or lines as motif.

In the early days, pure gold was used, creating a thick and rich lustre. After the Republic, it was replaced by foreign gold having a greenish tinge, which is darker in tone and tarnishes in time. Attention should be paid to the colour in authentication.

The painting style gave a three-dimensional effect and saw a marriage between Chinese and Western art, combining Western painting technique with the Lingnan School Style (嶺南畫法).

清代**廣彩碟**

A dish decorated with guangcai. Qing dynasty.

A jar decorated with guangcai. Qing dynasty.

清代**廣彩罐**

114

Unusual Vases Of Qing Dynasty

During the late Qing dynasty, there was a very unusual category of carved vase with motifs of flowers and colourful butterflies. In the Guangxu period, porcelain wares were carved with patterns, which were then filled with pale ink. Such porcelain wares were also found in the Qianlong period.

The enamelled vases have basically the same shape. Among the common ones are the *dan* vase, long-necked vase, broad-mouth vase, *guan yin* (Buddha) vase and *yu hu chun* vase. The hexagonal vase and the twin-bodied vase belong to two rather unique categories.

As for glazes, blue-and-white, *fencai*, underglazed red and *wucai* are attractive. So are the bean green, rouge red, tea dust, peachy red, sacrificial blue and peacock blue glazes.

Another noteworthy porcelain is one decorated with crab-shell green glaze. Some have carvings of flowers and birds on the walls; others are imitations of pre-Tang jade in the shape of *panchi* (蟠螭). Some Qing dynasty wares are imitations of lacquer vessels. Decorative carving was done, then the potter glazed and fired them with red pigment, after which, a second firing was made at a lower temperature, resulting in that lacquer-like appearance.

清乾隆**茶葉末釉瓶**，罕有。

A rare vase decorated with tea-dust glaze. Qianlong.

A vase decorated in a glaze with unstable colours. Yongzheng.

清雍正**窰變**
釉盤口瓶

Authentication of Whiteware of Early Qing

Antique porcelain is different in different periods. Dating and authenticating a ware just by form is difficult, but this can be an important criterion.

Ware of the Kangxi period has very fine clay yet its form is archaic, dignified and simple. It has perfect body-and-glaze fusion, and a powdery or starchy white surface.

Many Kangxi jars have a common earthern jar form. Still many have small variations in shape, such as the melon-shaped jar or the human-head-shaped jar. Some of them have an unglazed part outside the mouth rim, straight covers, or taper off under the belly. Fakes lack the glaze surface, foot, clay quality and stylistic variation.

Some whitewares from the popular kilns in early Qing have, on the mouth rim and the foot, a layer of powdery white glaze, giving them a thick quality, yet they normally have a natural fluffy edge and some broken bubbles.

New fakes look glossy and smooth. An original whiteware of the early Qing period has a firm and hard glaze on its mouth and foot; fakes have a loose and rough surface.

Statue of a handsome couple in whiteware from the Dehua kiln. Yongzheng. H: 17cm.

清雍正德化窰
白瓷才子佳人像，
高17厘米。

清初德化窰
白瓷觀音像，
高49.5厘米。

Statue of guan yin in whiteware. Early Qing, Dehua kiln. H: 49.5cm.

Coral-Red Porcelain

Coral-red porcelain was a new low-temperature ware produced in the early Qing. First available in the Kangxi period, it became popular in the Yongzheng and Qianlong periods. Its special feature is the red colour with a tinge of yellow. It is so called because of its coral-like colour.

Besides the monochrome coral-red bowl, vase, dish, saucer and jar of the period, there was one that used the coral-red colour as the ground colour and merged it with other colour enamels, creating various new glazed wares. Examples are the coral-red ground *wucai* and the coral-red ground *sancai* (三彩) ware.

Potters of the Yongzheng period also used coral-red as a ground colour for wares. One that stood out was the coral-red *fencai* - an exquisite ware with fine form, decoration and potting skill rarely seen today.

By the Qianlong period, the coral-red ware took on various forms. Some pieces were decorated with streaked gold and others were used as ornamental pieces.

After the Jiaqing period, it became scarce. The gold-streaked pieces were occasionally available but lacked the quality and craftsmanship of the first three periods.

The coral-red porcelain declined in production and quality during the Daoguang period. They had heavy, porous body and stiff motifs.

By the Tongzhi period, there was still no sign of a revival of this art ; the plethora of popular wares being rough pieces with liveless designs. The exceptions were a few official wares and pieces made specially for wealthy families. Common motifs of these wares are the characters *xi* (喜), fortune and longevity, red bat, hundred butterflies, and dragon-and-phoenix. Their prices are also lower than wares of the early Qing.

清代康熙**珊瑚紅地琺瑯彩花卉紋盌**一對。
「康熙御製」款，直徑10.7厘米。

A pair of bowls decorated in opaque enamels and coral-red ground with flowers. Qing dynasty, Kangxi mark and period. DM:10.7cm.

清代乾隆**天藍地浮雕纏枝壽桃瓶**。

A sky-blue vase decorated with carving in high relief of longevity peaches. Qianlong.

A sweet-white monk's cap ewer decorated with incised pattern of flowers. Early Ming dynasty. H: 19cm.

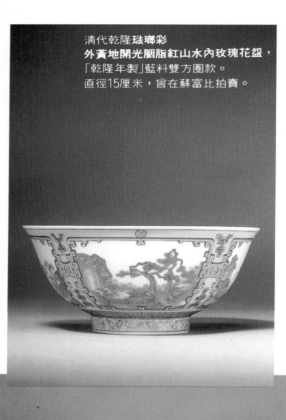

清代乾隆**琺瑯彩**
外黃地開光胭脂紅山水內玫瑰花盌，
「乾隆年製」藍料雙方圈款。
直徑15厘米，曾在蘇富比拍賣。

A yellow-ground, opaque-enamelled bowl decorated with landscape and roses in panels. Qing dynasty, Qianlong mark and period in double square. DM:15cm. Featured in one of Sotheby's auctions.

A yellow-ground opaque-enamelled bowl with flowers. Qianlong. DM: 15cm.

清代乾隆
黃地琺瑯彩花卉紋盌，
直徑15厘米。

A small bowl in opaque enamels
decorated with bamboo and
rose. Qing dynasty, Yongzheng
mark and period. DM:6.4cm.
Featured in one of Sotheby's
auctions.

清代雍正**琺瑯彩竹枝玫瑰題詩小盃**，
「雍正年製」藍料款。直徑6.4厘米，
曾在蘇富比拍賣。

A fencai large dish
decorated with plum
and peony. Yongzheng.
DM: 51cm.

清代雍正**粉彩
梅花牡丹紋大碟**，
直徑51厘米。

清代乾隆豆青釉
浮雕纏枝蓮花紋瓶，
曾在蘇富比拍賣。

A bean-green vase with lotus scrolls in relief. Qianlong. Featured in one of Sotheby's auctions.

清代乾隆**十蝠雀盃**。

A watercup with of ten
bats. Qianlong.

清代光緒**金魚雀盃**（民窰）。

A watercup with gold fish from a
popular kiln. Guangxu.

123

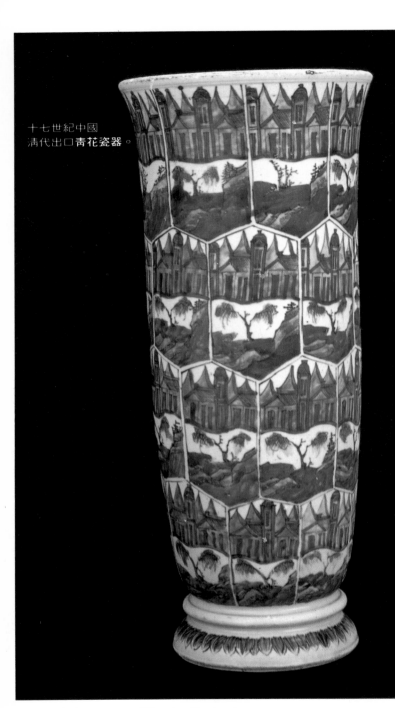

十七世紀中國
清代出口青花瓷器。

A blue-and-white export vase. 17th century Qing dynasty.

124

A lobed vase decorated with even-coloured glaze and pumpkin body. Qianlong. H: 21.3cm.

Chronology of Chinese History

夏	Xia	2100 – 1600 BC
商	Shang	1600 – 1100 BC
周	Western Zhou	1100 – 771 BC
春秋	Spring & Autumn Annals	770 – 476 BC
戰國	Warring States	475 – 221 BC
秦	Qin	221 – 206 BC
漢	Han	206 BC – AD 220
三國	Three Kingdoms	220 – 280
晉	Jin	265 – 420
南北朝	Southern & Northern	420 – 581
隋	Sui	581 – 618
唐	Tang	618 – 906
五代十國	Five Dynasties And Ten Kingdoms	907 – 960
宋	Sung	960 – 1279
元	Yuan	1279 – 1368
明朝	**Ming Dynasty**	1368 – 1643
洪武	Hongwu	1368 – 1399
建文	Jianwen	1399 – 1403
永樂	Yongle	1403 – 1424
洪熙	Hongxi	1425 – 1426
宣德	Xuande	1426 – 1435
正統	Zhentong	1436 – 1450
景泰	Jingtai	1450 – 1457
天順	Tianshun	1457 – 1465
成化	Chenghua	1465 – 1487
弘治	Hongzhi	1488 – 1505
正德	Zhengde	1506 – 1521
嘉靖	Jiajing	1522 – 1566
隆慶	Longqing	1567 – 1572
萬曆	Wanli	1573 – 1619
呑昌	Taichang	1620 – 1621
天啓	Tianqi	1621 – 1627
崇禎	Chongzhen	1628 – 1643
清朝	**Qing Dynasty**	1644 – 1912
順治	Shunzhi	1644 – 1661
康熙	Kangxi	1662 – 1722
雍正	Yongzheng	1723 – 1735
乾隆	Qianlong	1736 – 1795
嘉慶	Jiaqing	1796 – 1820
道光	Daoguang	1821 – 1850
咸豐	Xianfeng	1851 – 1861
同治	Tongzhi	1862 – 1874
光緒	Guangxu	1875 – 1908
宣統	Xuantong	1909 – 1912
中華民國	**Republic of China**	1912 – 1949
中華人民共和國	**People's Republic of China**	1949 –

Reign Marks of the Ming and Ching Dynasties

Yongle
1403-1424

Yongle
1403-1424

Xuande
1426-1435

Chenghua
1465-1487

Hongzhi
1488-1505

Zhengde
1506-1521

Jiajing
1522-1566

Longqing
1567-1572

Wanli
1573-1619

Tianqi
1621-1627

Chongzhen
1628-1643

Shunzhi
1644-1661

Kangxi
1662-1722

Yongzheng
1723-1735

Qianlong
1736-1795

Jiaqing
1796-1820

Daoguang
1821-1850

Xianfeng
1851-1861

Tongzhi
1862-1874

Guangxu
1875-1908

Xuantong
1909-1912

LEE YING HO • 李英豪

JADEITE

保值翠玉

Translator
Goh Beng Choo
An Asiapac Publication

100 Series Art Album

100 Celebrated Chinese Women

Artist Lu Yanguang captures the spirit
of some of China's most influential and
famous women. Spanning over two
thousand years of China's history, the
characters in this collection reflect the
many and varied roles which women
have played throughout the ages.

100 Chinese Gods

Lu Yanguang has interpreted Chinese
gods, goddesses and immortals with
imagination and intelligence.

A comprehensive range is represented:
from the superior Jade Emperor to the
fearsome King Yama of Hell; from the
compassionate Midwife Goddess to the
ordinary men who through practising
Taoism attained immortality and joined
the ranks of Heaven.

古董瓷器

著者：李英豪
翻譯：吳明珠

亞太圖書有限公司出版